Getting **Familiar** with the **Unfamiliar** 2

Understanding Unfamiliar Text Through Close Reading: NCEA Level Two

Kathryn **Fitzgerald** and
Tania Roxborogh

Getting Familiar with the Unfamiliar 2
1st Edition
Kathryn Fitzgerald
Tania Roxborogh

Cover designer: Cheryl Smith, Macarn Design
Text designer: Cheryl Smith, Macarn Design
Production controller: Siew Han Ong

Any URLs contained in this publication were checked for currency during the production process. Note, however, that the publisher cannot vouch for the ongoing currency of URLs.

For product information and technology assistance,
in Australia call **1300 790 853**;
in New Zealand call **0800 449 725**

For permission to use material from this text or product, please email **aust.permissions@cengage.com**

National Library of New Zealand Cataloguing-in-Publication Data
A catalogue record for this book is available from the National Library of New Zealand

978 0 17 042454 7

Cengage Learning Australia
Level 7, 80 Dorcas Street
South Melbourne, Victoria Australia 3205

Cengage Learning New Zealand
Unit 4B Rosedale Office Park
331 Rosedale Road, Albany, North Shore 0632, NZ

For learning solutions, visit **cengage.co.nz**

Printed in China by 1010 Printing International Limited.
8 9 25

Contents

When you see this icon, we want you to use at least one 'because' in your answer. The word 'because' is a magic word, as it forces you to explain and justify your statements.

When you see this icon, it means it is a term you might be unsure of, so we have included a definition in the glossary.

ISBN: 9780170424547

INTRODUCTION FOR TEACHERS

We have created this workbook for students to use with little or no teacher intervention, however, it would also be a great resource in the classroom. We expect that, taken as a series of lessons, texts 1 and 2 of each section would take two to three hours *each* to work through thoroughly as a class. Hopefully, you can see the benefit in breaking down the texts like this, and you are welcome to use this structure as a blueprint to create your own resources for unfamiliar texts.

As well as teaching close reading of unfamiliar texts, this book is also a great resource to use in the classroom for a range of the NCEA standards.

We have selected texts that:

- are exemplars of excellent writing (fiction and non-fiction)
- engage students in their study of poetry
- provide lots of practice at identifying and decoding language techniques/features
- teach students how to go 'beyond the text' and learn effective strategies to analyse texts
- in the non-fiction section, could be a springboard for Information Literacy
- have proved effective in teaching students strategies for how to produce better personal reading responses.

Recommended reading

Teaching Reading Comprehension Strategies by Sheena Cameron. This is a practical classroom guide that will expand on some of the techniques we use in this workbook.

INTRODUCTION FOR STUDENTS

Congratulations! By opening this book you have taken a big step in improving your understanding of reading unfamiliar texts. Whether you find understanding what you read a challenge or you want to learn how to effectively analyse how a text is constructed, this book is for you.

The aim of this book is to help you recognise patterns in a text and to understand and practise using reading tools so that not only will you feel more confident going into the end-of-year exam, but you will also have gained skills for more effective comprehension when faced with any unfamiliar text in the future.

In each section, the first two texts will have lots of activities that will help you understand the key parts of answering a Level 2 NCEA English question:

1. What do the words **say**? (definition of the words)
2. What do the words **mean**? (interpretation of the words)
3. **How** have the words been used? (identifying techniques)
4. **Why** have the words been used? (purpose or author's intent)

As you work through each section, you will see that the strategies and activities are gradually withdrawn until finally, at the end of each section, there are two texts that are presented in a similar way to those in the exam.

One of the most daunting things in the unfamiliar text exam is that sometimes you don't understand some, or many, of the words that are in the text and in the question. Because of this, where we deem it necessary, the first activity will be a vocabulary one. We can't guarantee that any of these words will be in the exam, but we are hoping that these activities will help to expand your own vocabulary.

ISBN: 9780170424547

We have been able to include only a small variety of ways to work with words you don't know and it is important that you realise there are other options. These will be things that you do most days without realising.

There are *seven key* strategies to help you approach words you don't know and they are:

1 Reread.
2 Read on.
3 Break down the word.
4 Use what you've already read to guess the meaning.
5 Use pictures, graphs, caption boxes, and/or photos around the text to look for clues.
6 Ask someone.
7 Check a dictionary.

It is good to be aware that there are deliberate strategies you can use to help you understand what you are reading, but obviously numbers 6 and 7 will not be available in the exam.

Let us show you how some of these strategies can be used

The section below is from a manual on how to change the oil filter of your car:

Before you head off to the auto parts store, consult your owner's manual for the type and weight of oil specific to your vehicle. It's especially important to follow the carmaker's recommendations for oil viscosity. That's a big change from the old DIY days. Late-model engines rely on oil pressure to regulate valve timing and apply the proper tension to the timing belt or chain. Substituting your personal preference for the manufacturer's recommendations can result in engine damage, poor performance and even a 'Check Engine' warning.

Source: https://www.familyhandyman.com/automotive/diy-oil-change/diy-car-maintenance-how-to-change-your-car-oil-yourself/view-all/

	Words I am unsure of	Strategy I used	How the strategy helped
1	viscosity	Use a dictionary. Ask someone.	I figured it had something to do with oil but I couldn't work it out from the context so I looked it up. The dictionary said the word means 'the state or property of being viscous', which still didn't really make sense so I asked my science teacher and she said it has to do with how easily the oil flows.
2	late-model	Use what I've already read to guess the meaning.	In the previous sentence, the writer talks about the 'old DIY days' so I am thinking the writer is talking about new cars.
3	timing belt	Look at the diagram. Read on.	The next word is 'chain' and I know that word so I looked at the picture and looked for something that was a chain. The illustration confirmed my understanding as the words 'timing belt' had an arrow to a chain in the picture.
4	regulate	Read on. Break down.	The sentence is talking about timing and I know the letters 're' mean to repeat or do again. It also reminds me of the word 'regulation', which I know has to do with rules (because of our school's uniform regulations) so I can guess this word means control or continuous control.
5	preference	Read on.	I see the sentence is talking about my ideas and the manufacturer's ideas. I understand the word 'substitute' means to replace so I'm guessing the writer is saying that if I stick with my ideas and don't change to what the maker of the car wants, I might damage my car. That would suck!

ISBN: 9780170424547

Now you have a turn:

Read the following paragraphs and use at least one of the strategies at the top of the previous page to figure out what the words mean. Try to use **reread**, **read on** or **break down the word**, as you won't be able to ask a friend or use a dictionary in the exam.

Apart from the Germans, the New Zealanders' biggest enemy on the Western Front was the mud. Indeed, the flooded trenches and churned landscape of the battlefields are among the most potent symbols of the First World War. This was particularly evident at Passchendaele, which was notoriously sodden due to the wet weather and the high water-table of this low-lying area, much of which was reclaimed marshland. Conditions were made much worse by the shelling, which had disrupted normal drainage.

Finding a dry spot to rest or sleep was often a challenge even though pumps were used to remove water from trenches and dugouts. Many troops succumbed to trench foot, a fungal infection caused by immersion in cold water. Rats and lice were soldiers' constant companions: rats, having gorged on corpses, allegedly grew 'as big as cats'; lice were the (then unknown) vector of another common wartime ailment, trench fever.

Source: https://nzhistory.govt.nz/war/new-zealanders-in-belgium/a-soldiers-lot

	Words I am unsure of	Strategy I used	How the strategy helped
1	churned		
2	Passchendaele		
3	notoriously		
4	water-table		
5	dugouts		

ISBN: 9780170424547

6	succumbed		
7	immersion		
8	gorged		
9	allegedly		
10	vector		

Now that you have learned about the seven deliberate reading strategies, try them out in your daily reading. When you see something you don't understand, don't give up but work through it using one or more of the strategies.

Completing this workbook will increase your chances of doing well in the unfamiliar text exam but don't underestimate the usefulness of reading something new every day and thinking about your response to it. Do you understand what the author is saying? Do you agree or disagree? Why? What response was the writer wanting from you and why?

The exam will cover narrative prose, poetry and non-fiction, so make sure you cover all these categories regularly in your reading.

We have designed this book so that you can either work through from start to finish or choose one of the sections that appeals to you and start there.

Good luck!

ISBN: 9780170424547

Section**One:** NARRATIVE PROSE

Narrative prose, known commonly as fiction, is probably the type of writing you are most familiar with, as you would have had stories read to you before you were even aware of what the written word was. Stories are always created for a purpose: to entertain, to inform, to persuade, to empathise, to teach ... the list is endless. The key for you, in terms of the unfamiliar text exam, is to recognise the purpose of the text you are reading.

To help you get there, we have designed the following activities around strategies such as looking at the title, the subject and the tone of the text. These are all strategies that you can take into the exam at the end of the year to help you formulate the answer to the question.

> *'I believe stories are incredibly important ... in allowing us to make sense of our lives, in allowing us to escape our lives, in giving us empathy and in creating the world that we live in.'*
>
> Neil Gaiman

NARRATIVE PROSE 1

Pre-reading activities

One of the most daunting things about the unfamiliar text exam is that sometimes you encounter words you don't understand. Because of this, we are including vocabulary activities and glossary definitions where we think it is necessary. We can't guarantee any of these words will be in the exam, but we are hoping that these activities will help to expand your vocabulary.

So, before you read this extract, let's prepare by looking at some words that might be new to you.

1 In the spaces below, write down the **literal** (dictionary) definition of the word and then, beside it, what ideas or feelings the word suggests to you (these suggestions are called **connotations**).

Word	Literal definition	Connotations
books		
second-hand		
bookshop		
dead/death		

2 What is the definiton of the word 'tending'?

____

____

3 Thinking about your answers to **1** and **2** above, what you do think might be the subject matter of the passage?

____

____

____

Reading the text

1 Read the text through once, slowly (out loud if you can). Don't do anything else; just read.

Tending the Books

Lives – dead ones – are just a hobby of mine. My real work is in the bookshop. My job is not to sell the books – my father does that – but to look after them. Every so often I take out a volume and read a page or two. After all, reading is looking after in a manner of speaking. Not old enough to be valuable for their age alone, nor important enough to be sought after by collectors, my charges are dear to me even if, as often as not, they are as dull on the inside as on the outside. No matter how banal the contents, there is always something that touches me. For someone now dead once thought these words significant enough to write them down.

People disappear when they die. Their voice, their laughter, the warmth of their breath. Their flesh. Eventually their bones. All living memory of them ceases. This is both dreadful and natural. Yet for some there is an exception to this annihilation. For in the books they write they continue to exist. We can rediscover them. Their humour, their tone of voice, their moods. Through the written word they can anger you or make you happy. They can comfort you. They can perplex you. They can alter you. All this, even though they are dead. Like flies in amber, like corpses frozen in ice, that which according to the laws of nature should pass away is, by the miracle of ink on paper, preserved. It is a kind of magic.

As one tends the graves of the dead, so I tend the books. I clean them, do minor repairs, keep them in good order. And every day I open a volume or two, read a few lines or pages, allow the voices of the forgotten dead to resonate inside my head. Do they sense it, these dead writers, when their books are read? Does a pinprick of light appear in their darkness? Is their soul stirred by the feather touch of another mind reading theirs? I do hope so. For it must be very lonely being dead.

From *The Thirteenth Tale* by Diane Setterfield, Orion Books, 2007.

2 What is your first impression of this passage?

Unpacking the text

1 IDENTIFY THE TONE

a Reread the text and:

i highlight, using different colours, positive words and negative words

ii circle words you don't know and look them up in a dictionary

iii underline words/phrases that stand out.

b i Identify the subject of the passage.

ii Write down a quote that *describes* (or *shows*) the subject of the passage.

How to identify tone

Basically, if the text has more positive than negative words = a positive tone. And, conversely, if it has more negative than positive words = a negative tone.

ISBN: 9780170424547

c Looking at your highlights, identify the dominant **tone** of the passage.

Some words we use to describe negative and positive tone:

Negative		**Positive**	
angry	sad	happy	joyful
resentful	afraid/scared	thankful	confident
uncertain	nervous	kind	funny

The tone is mostly ____________________ because of words such as ________________________________

____

d Describe the writer's attitude to the subject. Use examples from the passage to support your answer.

The writer is ______________________________ because she uses words like ____________________

______________________________ when discussing ____________________________

____

____.

2 FIND THE PATTERN

Each paragraph contains a central idea that relates to the overall purpose of the passage. The writer is 'building' her argument about the value of books by developing the images and explanations. Think of the passage as a jigsaw, in that each paragraph is a piece that connects to the pieces that come before and after. Looking at the individual pieces is part of what we call **unpacking the text and is a key skill in analysing**.

a In this task we want you to look at each paragraph by itself and summarise the idea – the jigsaw piece – in one sentence. We would also like you to jot down your own opinion as to what you think of the idea.

In one sentence, summarise a key idea from each paragraph.

Paragraph 1: ____

____

My opinion(s) on this idea: ____

____

Paragraph 2: ____

____

My opinion(s) on this idea: ____

____

Paragraph 3: ____

____

My opinion(s) on this idea: ____

____

ISBN: 9780170424547

b What is it you think the writer wants us to learn/know/understand about the value of reading and writing? Why do you think she believes it is important that we know this? You can use our suggested sentence starters or write your own.

The writer wants us to understand that books are important because ____________________

____

and that it's important we understand this so that/because ____________________

____

____

____

____________________.

Identifying how the text is communicated

We have deliberately waited until near the end of your analysis to get you to identify techniques. This is because at Level 2 it is crucial that you **understand the ideas** in the passage in detail prior to understanding **how** they are communicated.

Identifying the **subject** and **tone** of the passage like you did in the earlier activities helps you understand the writer's purpose. This purpose is then communicated through a variety of **language features** or **language techniques**. These terms are used interchangeably in this book.

Complete the following grid of **language features/techniques**. We have done some of it for you.

Technique	Example(s)	Why it is effective	How does this develop our understanding of the writer's purpose?
simile	like flies in amber like corpses frozen in ice	*Paints an image of objects getting preserved physically so that you can relate that to mental ideas of writing being preserved in books.*	*She is wanting us to recognise how everlasting/permanent people's words are, especially if they are printed in books. This preservation adds to the value of what is contained in the books but also shows how valuable are the people who wrote the words. Their words are like monuments that are erected publicly to honour famous/important people.*
adjective	dreadful		
rhetorical question	Do they sense it, these dead writers, when their books are read?		

ISBN: 9780170424547

Technique	Example(s)	Why it is effective	How does this develop our understanding of the writer's purpose?
personal pronoun			
listing			

Putting it all together

Most questions at this level ask you to 'analyse'. Let's first take a moment to understand what a question like this is asking you to do.

ANALYSE

This means discussing **WHAT? HOW? WHY?** and **SO WHAT** (are we to do/think as a result)?

So, look at:

- Selection of detail (the what),
- Use of techniques (how). Look back to the language features you've identified. Which ones help you to understand the 'what'?
- The way words and images are structured (effect). This is where our earlier strategies will be helpful.

It is useful to annotate the question to remind yourself to address each aspect in your answer. We have done this for you this time:

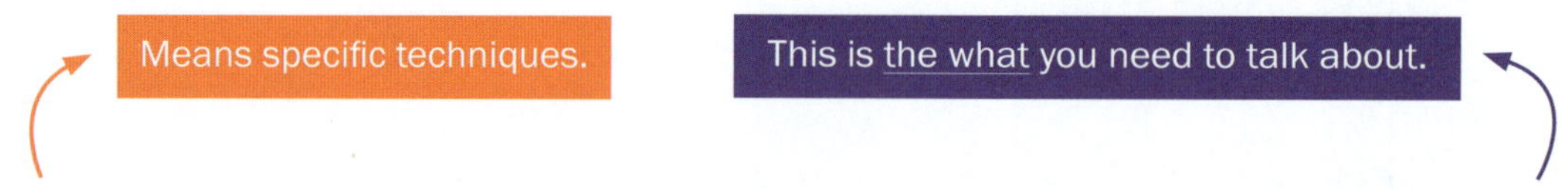

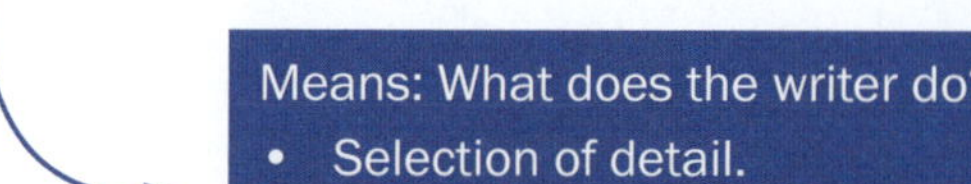

ISBN: 9780170424547

QUESTION

Analyse how the writer describes the narrator's role as a worker in a second-hand bookshop.

In your answer you should include examples of techniques used in the text, and explain their effects. (These might include, but are not limited to: repetition, personal pronouns, contrast, adjectives.)

You should start your answer using the words of the question. If you are stuck, you can use some of the starter sentences below to help you.

- *The writer describes the narrator's role as a worker in a second-hand bookshop as ...*
- *Her attitude towards this work is ...*
- *One way we see this is by the use of [insert technique], for example [insert quote], which is effective because [explain the effect of the technique], as it helps us understand ...*
- *Another way the writer shows this attitude to the role of a second-hand bookshop worker is by the use of [insert technique] and the use of insert [technique] when she writes [insert quote] and [insert quote].*
- *These techniques together emphasise the idea of ... because [describe effect of the techniques].*
- *Setterfield wants the reader to consider/think about/understand the idea or message [describe a key theme] because she wants us to [describe what action she wants from the reader].*

Structure:
A possible structure for your answer:
'The writer describes the narrator's role through the use of ____________________.'
(Name your technique, provide your evidence, explain the effect, link back to purpose. Repeat this for a second and then a third technique.)

ISBN: 9780170424547

NARRATIVE PROSE 2

Pre-reading activities

1 VOCABULARY WORK

Look up the following terms and write the most common meaning for each.

a human rights: ______________________________

____

b mainstream: ______________________________

____

c plastered (plaster): ______________________________

____

d anecdote: ______________________________

____

2 THE TITLE

The title of a text tells us a lot about the subject matter and/or the writer's purpose. It is worth spending some time thinking about what the title might mean before you read the piece.

This piece is called **We're Only Joking**.

G

a In the spaces below, write down the **literal** (dictionary) definition of the word and then, beside it, what ideas or feelings the word suggests to you (these suggestions are called **connotations**).

Word	Literal definition	Connotations
We're		
Only		
Joking		

b Look back at the definitions from the vocabulary work and combined with your answers above, finish this sentence:

I think this story might be about ______________________________

____

because ______________________________

____

____

______________________________.

The magic 'because'
The word 'because' is a magic word as it forces us to explain and justify our statements.

Reading the text

1 Read the text through once, slowly (out loud if you can). Don't do anything else; just read.

We're Only Joking

I see him walking outside the river of young adults, a lone wolf. He's dressed in trademark black, looking down at the ground. His heavy-duty headphones cover his head while his army-style boots create mushrooms of dust at the edge of the path. Each footstep falls within two metres of the mainstream, but the slightly chubby boy might as well be on Mars; he wouldn't be any closer to being normal.

The day has blurred by and I'm sitting two rows from the back of the bus. Roger sits at the rear, right in the middle of a fierce argument with Claire.

'Look, I've worked out how to solve all the problems in Africa,' he calls out with a crazy smile. 'Just kill all the little Africans!'

This generates passionate explosions of 'human rights' and 'how could you say that?!' from Claire. Roger roars with laughter and continues his theory on stopping world hunger.

'Roger, you're so weird and you have no friends,' spits Blake.

'I don't give a shit,' Roger replies through a plastic grin. It sounds convincing enough and has the desired effect on Blake, who turns around and leaves him alone for a bit. Roger's smile is still plastered to his face. It's actually a fairly accurate copy of the real thing, but the way it stays, without fading, betrays his true feelings. Over the long years of his life as an outcast, he has almost managed to convince himself that he doesn't care.

At school I'm sitting at a table with five other boys and stories of varying degrees of humour have been exchanged. Now it's my turn and my mind is racing to find an anecdote that will get a few laughs. My mind turns to Roger and the story of yesterday's bus trip begins. Sure enough, I get a few laughs and I'll admit, I found it funny too. But deep down I knew I was only burying Roger deeper.

The news comes as I'm waiting for the bus the next day. Roger's leaving school. False happiness cakes my face. 'Good,' I mutter, 'no more of those weird noises, eh?' Inside, a small part of me has broken. Not enough to make me feel upset for long, but enough to make me think.

Roger is gone. A young wolf kicked out of his pack to roam the forest alone. I won't see him again and part of me is happy; it's good we've finally gotten rid of him. He was weird. Wasn't he?

All those years, all those times when it was 'only a joke'. All of us thinking 'I'm only one person, what harm can I do?' Like a pitiless python, our laughter wrapped itself around Roger, its bright poisonous scales warning others away and squeezing him out of our lives.

Finn Lee, Year 12, 2013 (edited and abridged)

2 Use the space below to record your first impressions of the text.

ISBN: 9780170424547

Unpacking the text

Read through the text again.

> **How to identify tone:**
> Basically, if the text has more positive than negative words = a positive tone. And, conversely, if it has more negative than positive words = a negative tone.

1 Identify the subject of the story.

____

2 Write down three quotes that describe the subject of the story.

a _______________

b _______________

c _______________

3 Read the text through a third time. This time, underline all of the words that have negative connotations.

4 With a different colour, underline all of the words with positive connotations.

5 Looking at your highlights, identify the dominant **tone** of the passage. (Circle on the list below.)

Some words we use to describe negative and positive tone:

Negative		**Positive**	
angry	sad	happy	joyful
resentful	afraid/scared	thankful	confident
uncertain	nervous	kind	funny

Linking the title with the end of the text

A trick to help you understand the overall purpose of a text is to read only the title and the last line(s) together and then consider this as the idea or event that has motivated the author to write their piece. It can also help you identify the tone or attitude of the writer towards the subject of their text.

1 Write down the title and the last line of the text.

____

____

____

2 When you read this as one sentence, what does it tell you about the attitude of the writer towards the subject of the text?

____

____

____

____

____

ISBN: 9780170424547

Identifying how the text is communicated

We have deliberately waited until near the end of your analysis to get you to identify techniques. This is because at Level 2 it is crucial that you **understand the ideas** in the passage in detail prior to understanding **how** they are communicated.

G Identifying the **tone** of the passage like you did in the earlier activities helps you understand the writer's purpose. This purpose is then communicated through a variety of **language features** or **language techniques**. These terms are used interchangeably in this book.

1 The following **language features/techniques** can be found in the text. Find and label on the text (on page 15) an example of each of the techniques in the box below. Refer to the glossary (at the back of the book) if you do not know these words.

extended metaphor	imagery	metaphor	adjective
personification	rhetorical question	simile	

2 Identify one metaphor (or the extended metaphor) in the text and describe its significance.

3 Identify one rhetorical question in the text and describe its effect on the reader.

Putting it all together

Let's take a moment to understand what the question is asking you to do.

ANALYSE

This means discussing **WHAT? HOW? WHY?** and **SO WHAT** (are we to do/think as a result)?

So, look at:

- Selection of detail (the what),
- Use of techniques (how). Look back to the language features you've identified. Which ones help you to understand the 'what'?
- The way words and images are structured (effect). This is where our earlier strategies will be helpful.

ISBN: 9780170424547

It is useful to annotate the question to remind yourself to address each aspect in your answer. Fill in the blanks in the annotation. Refer to the annotated question on page 12 if you need help.

Means ______________________________

This is the ____________________ you need to talk about.

Analyse how the narrator feels about his part in Roger's decision to leave school.

Means: What does the writer do?

- ______________________________
- ______________________________
- ______________________________

QUESTION

Analyse how the narrator feels about his part in Roger's decision to leave school.

In your answer you should include examples of techniques used in the text, and explain their effects. (These might include, but are not limited to: metaphor, simile, personal pronouns, adjectives, rhetorical question.)

Structure:
The writer communicates his feelings about his part in Roger's decision to leave school through the use of ____________________. (Name your technique, provide your evidence, explain the effect, link back to purpose. Repeat this for a second and third technique.)

You should start your answer using the words of the question. If you are stuck, you can use some of the starter sentences below to help you.

- *The writer is feeling ... about his part in Roger's decision to leave school.*
- *He communicates this through the use of ...*
- *We see this technique in the quote '[insert quote]'.*
- *The effect of this is ... because ...*
- *This helps us understand Lee's overall purpose of ... because ...*
- *Another technique used to help us understand the narrator's feelings is ... This is used when he says '[insert quote]'.*
- *This helps us to understand he feels ...*
- *This links to the purpose because ...*
- *A final technique which helps us understand the narrator's feelings is ...*
- *We see this when Lee says '[insert quote]'.*
- *Lee wants the reader to consider/think about/understand the idea or message [describe a key theme] because she wants us to [describe what action she wants from the reader].*

____

____

____

____

____

____

____

ISBN: 9780170424547

NARRATIVE PROSE 3

Now that you have worked through two texts, we will be starting to remove some of the activities. This doesn't mean that they are no longer important, but, rather, we are hoping that you are starting to work through them naturally yourself as you read the text. Remember to pay attention to the language used, the title, and your first impressions.

Reading the text

1 Read the text through once, slowly (out loud if you can). Don't do anything else; just read.

All We Shall Know

There was a day on a beach long ago. There was sun and it was low in the sky and there was a warm breeze from the ocean. There was a spray on my face from the breaking waves and the tide was coming in but still there was a mile of beach and my mother was barefoot on it and my father's trouser legs were rolled up to his knees and he was holding a kite above his head with one hand and he was backing into the breeze and my mother was smiling, I think, in the shadow of her hat's wide brim, and she was saying, Go on, let go of it, it'll fly, it'll fly, come on while there's a steady breeze.

And my father half turned to look at me at the water's edge and he shouted, Watch this, Melody, and he let go and the kite lifted skyward as he let the reel out quickly and smoothly, and the kite, pink and purple and shaped like a butterfly, with long streamers of blue and gold, danced left and right in a shifting wind before tumbling suddenly downwards, into the wet sand.

For God's sake, Michael, my mother said. You have to keep the string taut, you have to keep moving.

And my father shouted that he'd be in the water if he kept going backwards, as he reeled in the string and lifted the kite to the sky again, and again the wind took it from his hand and he moved along the waterline ankle-deep in foam and the kite soared and the streamers trailed along the evening sky and again the kite was grabbed by some invisible hand and flung towards the ground, where it rested in a tidal pool, its streamers snaked around it. And my mother said, Oh, Michael. And I stood equidistant between them and I watched my father's reddening face as he rewound the string and untangled the streamers from the butterfly's wings and hoisted its flimsy body to the wind once more and watched as it swooped left and right and he tried to tauten the string and to match the kite's switching trajectories to keep it aloft and it crashed again into the sand and my mother said, Oh, forget it, forget it. And she said, Come on, Melody, and she put her hand out to me and when I took it she looked down at me and her eyes were shining and she laughed softly and said, Your poor father, and we turned for the steps to the car park. And I looked back at Daddy, who was still at the water's edge, facing the setting sun, and I saw him snap the butterfly's spine across his knee and toss its broken body to the waves.

From *All We Shall Know* by Donal Ryan, Doubleday, 2016.

2 Use the space below to record your first impressions of the text.

ISBN: 9780170424547

Unpacking the text

1 Identify the subject of the story.

____

2 Write down three quotes that describe the subject of the story.

a _______________

b _______________

c _______________

3 Read the text through again. This time, underline all of the words that have negative connotations.

4 With a different colour, underline all of the words with positive connotations.

5 Looking at your highlights, identify the dominant **tone** of the passage. (Circle on the list below.)

Some words we use to describe negative and positive tone:

Negative		**Positive**	
angry	sad	happy	joyful
resentful	afraid/scared	thankful	confident
uncertain	nervous	kind	funny

Identifying the 'point of change'

All fiction (narrative prose and poetry) has a 'point of change' in it. The point of change shows us the writer's **attitude** towards the subject, which helps understand the writer's purpose. Identifying and understanding the point of change is a **key to analysing the text**.

1 Reread the description of the first time Melody's father gets the kite into the air and then **compare** this with the description after it has crashed for the second time and then third time.

First time	Second and third time

2 How has the tone changed? Why?

The tone has changed from a _______________ description of flying a kite to _______________

_______________. I think this is because

____

____

____

_______________.

Inference is when we read between the lines of a text and make assumptions about what the deeper meanings might be based on the information we have been given. Now you have recognised the point of change, you are able to make some inferences about the story.

G

3 What can we **infer** about the relationship between Melody's parents from this story? Include at least one quote to back up your inference.

4 How might the kite symbolise what is going on between Melody's parents?

5 Melody is described as being 'equidistant' (at equal distance) between her parents. What can we infer about the impact this situation has on Melody?

ISBN: 9780170424547

Identifying how the text is communicated

G

Identifying the **subject**, **tone** and **point of change** of the text like you did in the earlier activities helps you understand the writer's purpose. This purpose is then communicated through a variety of **language features** or **language techniques**. These terms are used interchangeably in this book.

Complete the following grid of **language features**. We have started it off for you.

Technique	Example(s)	Why it is effective	How does this develop our understanding of the writer's purpose?
parallel structure	There was a day ... There was sun ... There was a spray ...		
	my mother my father I she he		
	The kite ... shaped like a butterfly		
adjective		Builds a very clear image in our minds of what Melody is seeing. It also helps us understand the tone as she starts off referring to everything in positive words and then changes to negative words as she picks up on her mother's negativity.	
repetition			
		Ryan uses little punctuation in this extract, which makes it feel like we are standing with Melody and watching the events unfold as she is.	
symbol			

Putting it all together

ANALYSE

This means discussing **WHAT? HOW? WHY?** and **SO WHAT** (are we to do/think as a result)?

Annotate the question to remind yourself to address each aspect in your answer. Refer to the annotated question on page 12 if you need help.

Analyse how the writer communicates Melody's experience at the beach.

QUESTION

Analyse how the writer communicates Melody's experience at the beach.

In your answer you should include examples of techniques used in the text, and explain their effects. (These might include, but are not limited to: structure; adjectives, parallel structure, symbol, personal pronouns.)

You should start your answer using the words of the question.
If you are stuck, you can use some of the starter sentences below to help you.

- *Melody's experience at the beach is ...*
- *The writer communicates this experience with the use of [insert technique].*
- *This change from ... to ... shows ...*
- *The effect of this [technique] is that it emphasises ...*
- *Through the kite the father shows that ...*
- *Melody feels ...*
- *This shows how ...*
- *Overall, Melody's experience at the beach is ...*
- *The writer wanted the reader to understand ...*

ISBN: 9780170424547

ISBN: 9780170424547

NARRATIVE PROSE 4

This is the final text in this section with some activities. Try to remember all of the strategies you have learned so far, even if they have been left out in this series of activities. In the exam you will have no activities and will rely on your memory to help you use the different strategies. It is good to start practising now.

Reading the text

1 Read the text through once, slowly (out loud if you can). Don't do anything else; just read.

Motueka Tobacco Farm, 1962

(Maiora Elder has just moved north to a Motueka tobacco farm. It is 1962.)

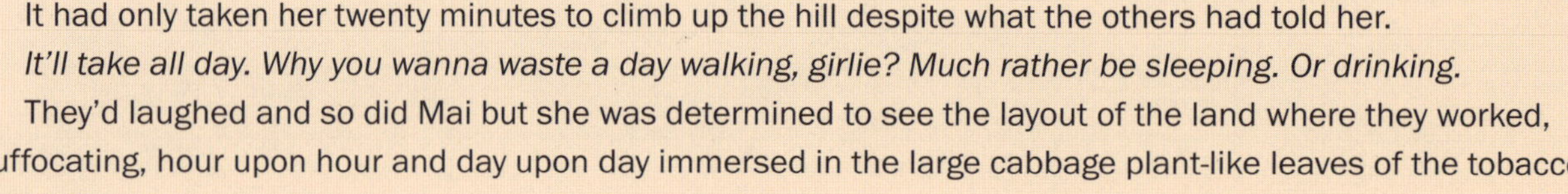

It had only taken her twenty minutes to climb up the hill despite what the others had told her.

It'll take all day. Why you wanna waste a day walking, girlie? Much rather be sleeping. Or drinking.

They'd laughed and so did Mai but she was determined to see the layout of the land where they worked, suffocating, hour upon hour and day upon day immersed in the large cabbage plant-like leaves of the tobacco plantation.

The grey-dust mountains in the distance surrounded the valley like a group of old *kaumātua*: silent, strong, reliable. The valley looked like the flat belly of an unevenly tanned sleeping man. The continuous working of the wind gently stroking the plants in the valley below imitating breathing, a dreamer shuddering. The image reminded her of the hay paddocks down on the farm.

Her ear caught snatches of music from far below. Someone had dragged the record player out into the yard but they only had one record between them so Mai anticipated the opening notes: *The tears I cry for you could fill an ocean*, sang Connie Francis. A discordant chorus joined in. *But you don't care how many tears I cry.*

Their laughter made a lie of the sad love song and she couldn't help but smile because that was all they talked about among the vines, at dinner and after dark: the men who had broken their hearts.

Which was the point of coming high up here today. Up here, away from the heat and the sweet smell of the tobacco plants, a smell that reminded her of when Mum's glasshouse was filled with flourishing tomato plants, she could breathe. And think more clearly and push away the dark clouds that sometimes filled her vision whenever she was down here or back home.

The song disappeared back toward the east and Mai spread out her cardigan and sat down. From her bag she pulled out an apple and the small pouch of yellow leaves she'd swiped from the packing shed. *Last year's crop*, the foreman had said. *No one's gonna miss it, girlie, but don't let me see you do it again.*

Her fingers, the nails bitten down but not uncomfortably so, were stained because yesterday she'd left her gloves behind under the bunk. She studied them, thinking of home, hearing the echo of her mother's voice. The tone of disapproval a consistent background song to her childhood. Mai looked for colour in her remembering and she thought of Aunty Shirl who always wore red lipstick and a bright yellow print-flower dress which she'd bought brand new at Ballantynes during the war. Mum always brought up the dress when issuing warning or caution about foolish and impulsive behaviour. *Look at your Aunty Shirl. Did as she pleased and now? No man and no children. Do you want to end up like her?*

Actually, Aunty Shirl's life appealed. She's got away from home and made a life for herself up north. Mum and Dad said she ran with a bad crowd. *Some Maori agitators in Wellington*, they said. *It would only end in tears.*

Being here, being with the other women, meeting Tom, discovering herself, Mai thought Aunty Shirl was on to something. Something free and something good even if it came with a possibility of pleasurable pain.

From *Motueka Tobacco Farm, 1962* by T.K. Roxborogh.

ISBN: 9780170424547

Unpacking the text

1 Read the text through again. Identify the subject of the passage. ______________________________

2 Pull out words that have negative and positive connotations (feelings and images we associate with them, rather than the literal meaning) and place them in the grid below.

Positive	Negative

3 What do you think is the overall **tone** of this passage and why? Give a quote from the passage to back up your opinion.

I think the tone is negative/positive (delete one). I see this in the passage when it says '______________________________

______________________________'. This makes the tone ______________________________

because ______________________________

____

____

______________________________.

4 Describe the writer's attitude to the subjects. ______________________________

____

____

Identifying how the text is communicated

Complete the following grid of **language features**.

Technique	Example(s)	Why it is effective	How does this develop our understanding of the writer's purpose?
simile		Because the mountains are being described as old, backward, traditional, watchful, like men ...	She feels trapped here in this place she's 'escaped' to and feels like her family are still watching her every move – judging
repetition	... **tears I cry** for you ... how many **tears I cry** ...	Emphasises the emotion of being sad.	

ISBN: 9780170424547

Technique	Example(s)	Why it is effective	How does this develop our understanding of the writer's purpose?
	red lipstick bright yellow print-flower dress		In contrast to the grey of the mountains which make Mai feel trapped, the memory of Aunty Shirl is positive and emphasises the idea that being different, radical, breaking away from the norms/restrictions of traditions is a positive thing.
personification		The mountain/plants are alive.	
listing	Being here, being with the other women, meeting Tom, discovering herself, ...	Makes more convincing by building up examples/by providing a number of reasons, adds weight.	
present continuous verb	**Being** here, **being** with the other women, **meeting** Tom, **discovering** herself, ...		

Putting it all together

ANALYSE

This means discussing **WHAT? HOW? WHY?** and **SO WHAT** (are we to do/think as a result)?

Annotate the question to remind yourself to address each aspect in your answer. Refer to the annotated question on page 12 if you need help.

Analyse how the writer reveals Mai's feelings as she looks out over her surroundings.

ISBN: 9780170424547

QUESTION

Analyse how the writer reveals Mai's feelings as she looks out over her surroundings.

In your answer you should include examples of techniques used in the text, and explain their effects. (These might include, but are not limited to: use of te reo Māori, simile, listing, adjectives, repetition.)

If you are stuck, look back over the sentence starters provided earlier in this book.

ISBN: 9780170424547

NARRATIVE PROSE 5

Now that you have completed the first four narrative prose text activities, you are ready to attempt a piece as if you were under exam conditions.

Using all the strategies you have been practising throughout this chapter, give this your best shot. Put your timer on for 20 minutes. Read the piece and use your strategies to answer the question. Good luck!

Aging Backwards

Mind far away, most likely forgetting his whereabouts and who surrounds him. Despite this he still looks comfortable laying on the chair. My dad gently prods his shoulder. 'Dad, tea?'

He opens his light grey eyes which are dusted with that layer of mist I have come to associate with old age. These colourless eyes, withered away by time are lost and disorientated for only a moment before he nods. My father's shoulders relax, Grandpa recognises him. I turn back to my book. Grandpa watches me for a moment, just a moment, before moulding to the chair like moss to a log.

He forgets who I am more each day. Like tiny pin pricks it pierces my heart, somewhat worse than having my heart wrenched out in one foul blow. I'm used to it now. But when he forgets my father, his own son, my body strains as it ices over. It's not his fault, but how can I not be frustrated.

Why does he put Dad through this pain? Can't he see my dad flinch when he gets his name wrong? Sadly, no. He is oblivious to the anguish he causes. All we can do is try and keep life normal for him. But nothing is normal when your mind is slowly decaying, rotting away without a hope of remission because there is no remedy to restore one's memory.

My father returns with a strong tea to find Grandpa dozing once more. His long arms lounge on the armrests of the glorious chair that we reserve for him. It used to belong to him, before he moved into a small retirement village where it would not fit. This chair is one familiar object in a house of unknowns.

He is a big man, strong shoulders as broad as a picture frame. A giant painting which now belongs in our home, a decoration, showing remains of what once was. White hairs provide a scarce cover over his head, particularly patchy parts reveal a speckled scalp. His plain trousers are hitched up revealing a section of his shin. Over the years, the muscle he once had has disappeared, slowly being replaced with wrinkled skin that hangs and droops off the bone as curtains.

'What book are you reading?'

I look up to Grandpa who sits awaiting an answer. I rise and carry my book to him. 'Oliver Twist,' I say handing the old copy over.

He studies the cover, which should be familiar considering he has read it 8 times. 'Do you mind if I have a read?' I shake my head and instead take myself over to the piano stool.

Grandpa was an English scholar and a linguist. Dickens was his favourite to read, and study. My dad always laughs when he recalls Grandpa attempting to read Oliver Twist in five languages. Supposedly he also wanted to read Oliver Twist in Latin, but there were no copies. I suspect there is no room in his head for all those languages anymore. His mind overcrowded from the 87 years spent on this Earth.

I stretch my fingers and place them on the glossy marble keys. I start the piece leisurely, full of finesse, allowing room to build up for a faster mid-section. Notes flow together filling the empty spaces of the room with melodic combinations and memories.

Only when I bring my playing down to the end do I realise he is singing, off key, but still singing. His voice glorious with the aches and struggles that time has granted him.

'Again, again!' he exclaims. I glance at my dad, who chuckles and I set off again playing to a captivated audience.

After what feels like a life time of playing and singing, full of merriment and mirth, comes time for Grandpa

ISBN: 9780170424547

to leave. My dad has to help him put on his jumper after he made an attempt to pull it on inside out. As Dad assists him into the car, I say goodbye. Grandpa beams at me, a touch of pink returned to his cheeks.

'English Country Gardens is my absolute favourite! Play it again for me next time would you?' I begin to reply, but his mind is already far away, forgetting his whereabouts and who surrounds him.

So all I do is nod and wave goodbye.

Lexi Richards, Year 12, 2017.

QUESTION

Analyse how the writer reflects on the impact of her grandfather's aging.

In your answer, you should include examples of techniques used in the text and explain their effects. (These might include, but are not limited to: rhetorical question, personal pronouns, adjectives, metaphor.)

ISBN: 9780170424547

NARRATIVE PROSE 6

Using all of the skills you have been practising throughout this chapter, give this your best shot. Put your timer on for 20 minutes. Read the piece and use your strategies to answer the question. Good luck!

Recognition

The house looks bigger; the bricks brighter, the windows clearer. Looking at the ground I see a mess of trodden grass, cigarette butts and dumped concrete. Here and there a Chupa Chups stick litters what is left of the front garden – perhaps one of the builders was trying to quit smoking.

I let my sister take my luggage from the car and decide to do a lap around the house before I go inside – to put off what could be exciting or disappointing but either way, a change and the first real sign that things have to move on.

As I go past the kitchen windows I pause, struggling to remember what plants were once where there is now only mud. This is not a new feeling for me; I drive down streets and pass vacant lots without even a glimmer of recognition. What *is* new is that I've attached that feeling to my own home – I never thought that could happen.

The side gate hangs awkwardly and with what appears to be fragility but when I push it, it refuses to move. It takes two hands and a shove and I'm able to get through the gap I create. The old kitchen windows are propped against the fence in the backyard. And over there, tucked out of sight like a stain, lies the kitchen itself. I think of my grandmother, who would have been full of joy when that kitchen was installed in 1958; and my grandfather, who hand painted it when old age and loneliness meant he couldn't sleep at night. What would they think, that same kitchen now tucked out of sight?

I continue my slow, solitary walk, noticing small things that have appeared, changed or vanished. Again, my memory searches clumsily to recall what was there but it is like sifting through glug. Everything looks so different on this grey winter's morning after 12 weeks away.

All too soon I circle back to the front door which is exposed, now that my grandfather's handmade wrought iron framework is slumped in the garden. Suddenly, my sister is loitering at my left elbow; her shrill voice and grinning face fill my vision. She can't wait to show me the changes, the improvements, which my parents and the builders have wrought on the house.

I struggle to share her enthusiasm. The house is old. I know that. And it is cold. In winter I sleep with a hoodie and beanie on to stave off the chill that seeps from the walls. But it is ours. My dad grew up here; my uncle's name is carved in childish writing on a brick on the back wall. My brother and uncle both celebrated their 21st birthdays in the garage – nearly 35 years apart. My grandmother passed away peacefully in the lounge before I was born. I composed my eulogy for my grandfather's funeral in a sunny patch in the garden on a spring morning. I'd always imagined I'd bring my baby home here; the fourth generation.

But the Christchurch earthquakes have sped up the inevitable. What is left of the garden my grandparents lovingly cultivated is unkempt. The gravel road they bought their home on is now a busy bus route. Heart-breaking aftershocks caused the kitchen to slump and large cracks to run through the brickwork. It meant builders, strangers, had to come into our home.

What I do recognise, finally, is that it's time to let go. Time to move on. I squeeze my eyes, look at my sister and follow her in to the house.

K. Ryan, 2013.

QUESTION

Analyse how the writer communicates her feelings about the change to her family home.

In your answer you should include examples of techniques used in the text, and explain their effects. (These might include, but are not limited to: listing, simile, sentence structure, word choice.)

ISBN: 9780170424547

Section Two: POETRY

Poems can be written to sound beautiful, to tell a story or share a message. They are designed to recreate the emotional response and/or experience of the poet for the reader. In analysing poetry, **how** the ideas are communicated is just as important as **what** the ideas are.

The poet specifically pays attention to:

- structure and rhythm
- form
- tone
- word choice
- all of the things that create the effect the poet is trying to achieve.

> *'To see (read) is to appreciate. To analyse is to understand (which often deepens our appreciation).'*
>
> Dr Greg Crossan, Massey University, 1986

One tip we would give you is to think about poems as icebergs – they can be enjoyed for their beauty if you see them just from the surface, but total appreciation of their scale and magnitude can only be successful when you dive down and look beneath.

POETRY 1

Pre-reading activities

1 THE TITLE

The title of a poem is often a **metaphor** and is a helpful clue to understand the poet's overall purpose for writing the poem. It is worth spending a bit of time working out what the title might mean.

The Trees is the title of your first poem.

a Use the below space to draw your visualisation of a tree. Surround the picture with words that you associate with the word 'tree' or 'trees'.

b In the spaces below, write down the **literal** (dictionary) definition of the word and then, beside it, what ideas or feelings the word suggests to you (these suggestions are called **connotations**).

The ____________________ ____________________

Trees ____________________ ____________________

2 PREDICTING

Looking at your ideas from above, predict **two different** words you think might appear in this poem. For each word, give a reason why you think this might be.

a ____________________ because ____________________

____

____________________.

b ____________________ because ____________________

____

____________________.

Reading the poem

1 Read the poem through once, slowly (out loud if you can). Don't do anything else; just read.

The Trees

The trees are coming into leaf
Like something almost being said;
The recent buds relax and spread,
Their greenness is a kind of grief.

Is it that they are born again
And we grow old? No, they die too.
Their yearly trick of looking new
Is written down in rings of grain.

Yet still the unresting castles thresh
In fullgrown thickness every May.
Last year is dead, they seem to say,
Begin afresh, afresh, afresh.

Philip Larkin

Poetry Diary 2013, Faber and Faber.

About this poem
Philip Larkin is an English poet. He wrote this poem in 1967. In England, May is the month of spring where things are born anew.

ISBN: 9780170424547

2 Use the space below to record your first impressions. You can write in bullet points, draw some images or write in full sentences.

3 Read the poem again. Pull out words that have negative and positive connotations (feelings and images we associate with them, rather than the literal meaning) and place them in the grid below.

Positive	Negative

G 4 What do you think is the overall **tone** of this poem and why? Give a quote from the poem to back up your opinion.

I think the tone of *The Trees* is negative/positive (delete one). I see this in the poem when it says '____'. This makes the tone ____________________

because ____.

Linking the title with the end of the poem

A trick to help you understand the overall purpose of a poem is to read only the title and the last line(s) together and then consider this as the idea or event that has motivated the poet to write their poem. It can also help you identify the tone or attitude of the poet towards the subject of their poem.

1 Write down the title and the last sentence of the poem.

2 What might the information above tell you about the poet's attitude towards life?

ISBN: 9780170424547

Unpacking the text

Think of the poem as a jigsaw, in that each section is a piece that connects to the pieces that come before and after. Looking at the individual pieces is what we call unpacking the text.

1 In this task, we want you to look at each **stanza** by itself and explain what is said by summarising the idea – the jigsaw piece – in one sentence. The first one has been done for you as an example.

Stanza	Summary
1	New leaves have sprouted on the trees, replacing the buds, which suggests that it is springtime.
2	
3	

2 SUMMARISE

a In no more than two sentences, write what this poem is about.

____

____

____

____

____

____

b Complete the following sentence. You should include a description of **what** the writer wants us to learn/know/understand about our world/about life and **why** we need to learn this.

The writer/speaker wanted to teach us about ______________________________

____

because ______________________________

____

____

____

______________________________.

ISBN: 9780170424547

Identifying the 'point of change'

All fiction (poetry and narrative prose) has a 'point of change' in it. The point of change shows us the writer's **attitude** towards the subject, which helps us understand the writer's purpose. Identifying and understanding the point of change is a strategy used to analyse the poem.

This poem is unusual in that it has two points of change. The first is a change in **atmosphere** and the second is a change in the **poet's understanding** of things.

1 Identify the line where the first point of change occurs. ______________________

2 Identify the line where the second point of change occurs. ______________________

3 Describe the atmosphere in the first section of the poem. ______________________

____

____

4 Identify two words that contribute to this atmosphere.

a ______________________ b ______________________

5 Describe what the poet realises after the first change.

____

6 Describe the tone of the poem after the second point of change.

____

7 Why do you think Larkin has included these changes?

____

____

____

Identifying how the poem is communicated

We have deliberately waited until near the end of your analysis to get you to identify techniques. This is because at Level 2 it is crucial that you **understand the ideas** in the poem in detail prior to understanding **how** they are communicated.

Identifying the **tone** and **point of change** of the poem like you did in the earlier activities helps you understand the poet's purpose. This purpose is then communicated through a variety of **language features** or **language techniques**. These terms are used interchangeably in this book.

1 The following **language features** can be found in the text. Find and label on the text (on page 35) six examples of from the list below. Refer to the glossary (at the back of the book) if you do not know these words.

simile	metaphor	rhyme	sibilance
personification	adjective	assonance	personal pronoun
repetition	alliteration	question	

2 Fill in the following grid about the ideas in the poem and what techniques help communicate these ideas – we have started it off for you.

Technique	Evidence	Effect	Purpose
question	Is it that they are born again/And we grow old?	Makes us stop and think and wait for the answer.	We reflect on our questioning about growing old and look to compare our answers with the poet.
alliteration	**gr**eenness ... **gr**ief **l**eaf/**L**ike **r**ecent buds **r**elax **s**eem to **s**ay	Draws attention to both words to set up a contrast between them.	
assonance	unr**est**ing ... thr**esh**	Emphasises the words and idea of movement.	
repetition	afresh, afresh, afresh	Shows how important the word is.	
sibilance		Makes a sound similar to the wind.	
rhyme scheme			To remind us that trees, like us, have a life cycle of beginnings and endings, that there is a circular nature of life.

Putting it all together

Let's first take a moment to understand what the question is asking you to do.

ANALYSE

This means discussing **WHAT? HOW? WHY?** and **SO WHAT** (are we to do/think as a result)?

So, look at:

- Selection of detail (the what),
- Use of techniques (how). Look back to the language features you've identified. Which ones help you to understand the 'what'?
- The way words and images are structured (effect). This is where our earlier strategies will be helpful.

ISBN: 9780170424547

It is useful to annotate the question to remind yourself to address each aspect in your answer. We have done this for you this time.

Means specific techniques.

This is the what you need to talk about.

Analyse how the writer compares the life cycle of trees to the life cycle of people.

Means: What does the writer do?

- Selection of detail.
- Use of techniques.
- Way words/images are structured.

QUESTION

Analyse how the writer compares the life cycle of trees to the life cycle of people.

In your answer you should include examples of techniques used in the text, and explain their effects. (These might include, but are not limited to: question, alliteration, assonance, sibilance, rhyme scheme.)

You should start your answer using the words of the question. If you are stuck, you can use some of the starter sentences below to help you.

- *The writer compares the life cycle of trees to the life cycle of people because ...*
- *Larkin uses [insert technique] when he says [insert quote from poem].*
- *This means ..., which makes us think about ...*
- *By personifying the ..., the poet is reminding us ... because ...*
- *The poet also uses [insert technique and specific example from the poem].*
- *He does this because ...*
- *The [insert technique and example] makes us think ...*
- *The reason for this is ...*
- *This is further emphasised with ...*
- *The purpose of this is to ensure we ...*
- *The whole poem is ...*
- *Larkin uses his reflections to [comment here about how the poem connects to your understanding of the world].*

Structure:
A possible structure for your answer:
'The writer compares the life cycle of trees to the life cycle of people through the use of ________________.
(Name your technique, provide your evidence, explain the effect, link back to purpose. Repeat this for a second and then a third technique.)

ISBN: 9780170424547

POETRY 2

Pre-reading activities

1 THE TITLE

The title of a poem is often a **metaphor** and is a helpful clue to understand the poet's overall purpose for writing the poem. It is worth spending a bit of time working out what the title might mean.

Anytime is Wrong Time and so is In-Between Time is the name of this poem.

a In the spaces below, write down the **literal** (dictionary) definition of the word and then, beside it, what ideas or feelings the word suggests to you (these suggestions are called **connotations**).

Word	Literal	Connotations
Anytime		
Wrong		
Time		
In-Between		

b What do you think the poem is going to be about? Don't forget a magic 'because'.

____

____

____

____

____

____

The magic 'because'
The word 'because' is a magic word as it forces us to explain and justify our statements.

ISBN: 9780170424547

Reading the poem

1 Read the poem through once, slowly (out loud if you can). Don't do anything else, just read.

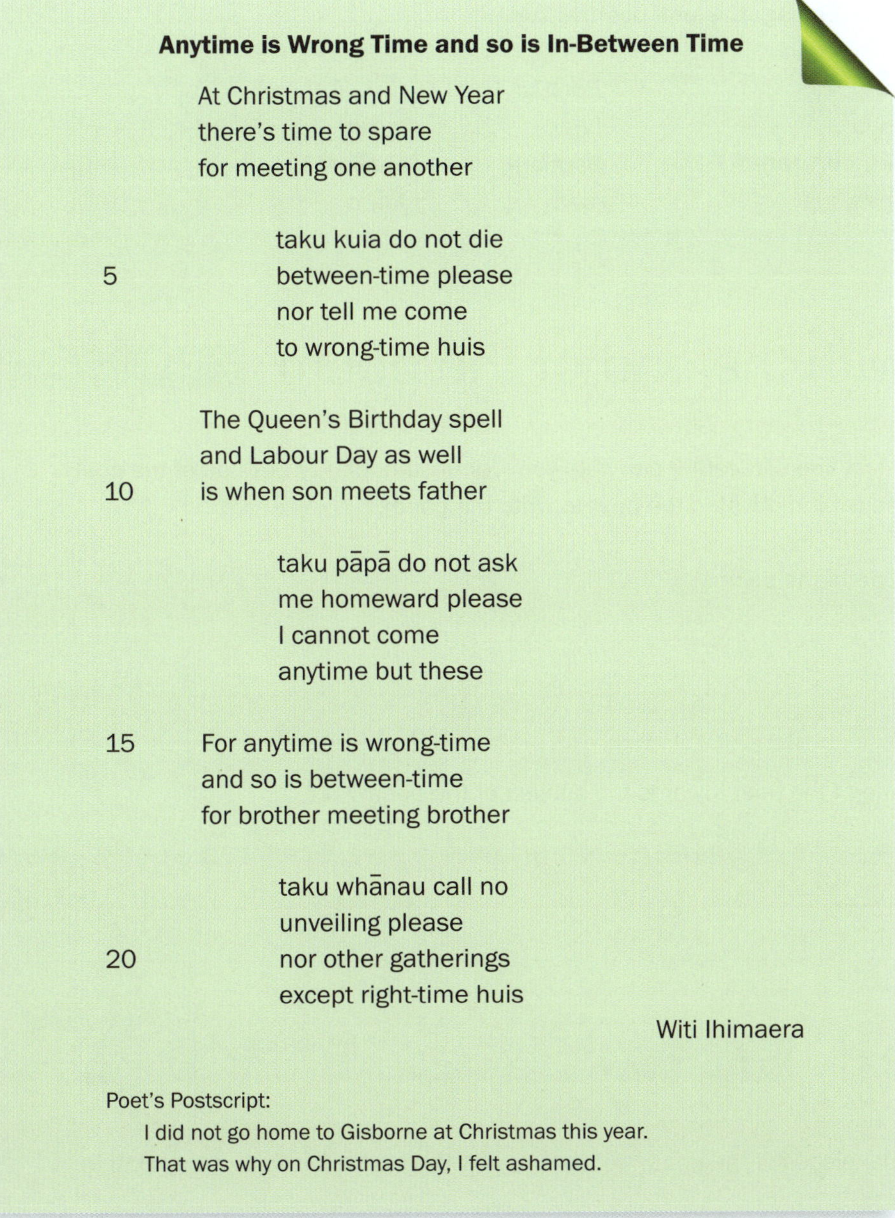

Anytime is Wrong Time and so is In-Between Time

At Christmas and New Year
there's time to spare
for meeting one another

taku kuia do not die
between-time please
nor tell me come
to wrong-time huis

The Queen's Birthday spell
and Labour Day as well
is when son meets father

taku pāpā do not ask
me homeward please
I cannot come
anytime but these

For anytime is wrong-time
and so is between-time
for brother meeting brother

taku whānau call no
unveiling please
nor other gatherings
except right-time huis

Witi Ihimaera

Poet's Postscript:
I did not go home to Gisborne at Christmas this year.
That was why on Christmas Day, I felt ashamed.

Pacific Voices, selected by Bernard Gadd, Macmillan Publishers New Zealand Ltd, 1989.

G

hui – meeting for a particular purpose (note that there is no plural in te reo Māori so there is a deliberate use of 's' in 'huis')
kuia – grandmother/older woman
pāpā – father
taku – mine
unveiling – to remove cover or shroud
whānau – family

2 Use the space below to record your first impressions of the poem. You can write in bullet points, draw some images or write in full sentences.

3 Read the poem through again. This time, underline all of the words that have negative connotations.

4 With a different colour, underline all of the words with positive connotations.

5 Looking at your highlights, identify the dominant **tone** of the passage. (Circle on the list below.)

Some words we use to describe negative and positive tone:

Negative		Positive	
angry	sad	happy	joyful
resentful	afraid/scared	thankful	confident
uncertain	nervous	kind	funny

Linking the title with the end of the poem

Remember, reading the title and the last line(s) together can help you identify the tone or attitude of the poet towards the subject of their poem and what motivated the poet to write the poem.

1 Write down the title and the last line of the poem.

____

____

____

2 What does it tell you about the tone of the poet towards the subject of the poem?

____

____

____

Unpacking the text

Remember, by looking at the individual pieces of the poem we can **unpack the text and this is a key skill in analysing**.

1 In this task we want you to look at each stanza by itself and summarise the idea – the jigsaw piece – in one sentence.

The poet is stuck between the Pākehā and Māori world. On the chart on the next page, identify which 'world' each stanza refers to. We would also like you to jot down your own opinion as to what you think of the idea in each stanza. We have done three for you to get you started.

ISBN: 9780170424547

Stanza	Summary	My opinion	Which world?
1	During public holidays there is time for catching up.	I agree with this; it is great that everyone is on holiday around the same time.	Pākehā
2			
3			
4	Doesn't want his pāpā to put pressure on him by asking him to come home.		Māori
5			
6	Doesn't want any funerals or gatherings at times that are not public holidays. He is happy for positive gatherings at times that suit him.		Māori

2 How do you think the poet feels about family gatherings and why?

The poet feels ______________________ about family gatherings because ______________________

______________________. We see this when the poet says

'[insert quote] ______________________.'

The author added an 's' to the Māori word 'hui' to make it plural even though this does not happen in te reo Māori. If it was being written today, this wouldn't happen but then the endings wouldn't rhyme!

3 Does rhyming matter? Which is more important, convention or tradition? Why?

____

____

____

____

____

____

____

____

ISBN: 9780170424547

Identifying the 'point of change'

The point of change shows us the writer's **attitude** towards the subject (topic of the poem), which helps understand the writer's purpose. Identifying and understanding the point of change is **a strategy used to analyse a poem**.

1 Identify the point of change in the poem according to the line number(s). ______________________

2 What are the connotations of the word 'except'? ______________________

____

3 What is the poet trying to tell us by this point of change?

____

____

____

4 What does this imply about working and family life?

____

____

____

Identifying how the poem is communicated

We have deliberately waited until near the end of your analysis to get you to identify techniques. This is because at Level 2 it is crucial that you **understand the ideas** in the poem in detail prior to understanding **how** they are communicated.

The following **language features** can be found in the text.

imperative	lack of punctuation	hyphenated word	use of proper noun
personal pronoun	use of te reo Māori	structure	repetition

1 Find and label on the text (on page 43) six examples of the techniques in the box above. Refer to the glossary (at the back of the book) if you do not know these words.

2 Complete the following grid of **language features**.

Technique	Example(s)	Effect
proper noun		As New Zealanders, we know that these are public holidays where most businesses are shut. These are holidays that are attached to the Pākehā world.
personal pronoun	me I	

Technique	Example(s)	Effect
	taku kuia taku pāpā taku whānau	Allows us to know that this poem is set in New Zealand and that the poet is of Māori heritage. It contrasts with the use of proper nouns in the odd stanzas.
structure	six stanzas: 1, 3 and 5 are three lines each and aligned to the margin; 2, 4 and 6 are four lines each and indented	
repetition		

Putting it together

Let's first take a moment to understand what the question is asking you to do.

ANALYSE

This means discussing **WHAT? HOW? WHY?** and **SO WHAT** (are we to do/think as a result)?

So, look at:

- Selection of detail (the what),
- Use of techniques (how). Look back to the language features you've identified. Which ones help you to understand the 'what'?
- The way words and images are structured (effect). This is where our earlier strategies will be helpful.

It is useful to annotate the question to remind yourself to address each aspect in your answer. Fill in the blanks in the annotation. Refer to the annotated question on page 40 if you need help.

Means ______________________

This is the ______________ you need to talk about.

Analyse how the writer communicates his feeling about going home.

Means: What does the writer do?

- ______________________
- ______________________
- ______________________

ISBN: 9780170424547

QUESTION

Analyse how the writer communicates his feelings about going home.

In your answer you should include examples of techniques used in the text, and explain their effects. (These might include, but are not limited to: structure, use of te reo Māori, personal pronouns, repetition.)

You should start your answer using the words of the question.
If you are stuck, you can use some of the starter sentences below to help you.

- *The writer communicates his feelings of … about going home.*
- *Ihimaera uses [insert technique] when he says [insert quote from poem] …*
- *This means …*
- *Which makes us think about …*
- *By personifying the …, the poet is reminding us … because …*
- *The poet also uses [insert technique and specific example from the poem] …*
- *He does this because …*
- *The [insert technique and example] makes us think …*
- *The reason for this is …*
- *This is further emphasised with …*
- *The purpose of this is to ensure we …*
- *The whole poem is …*
- *Ihimaera uses his reflections to [comment here about how the poem connects to your understanding about the world].*
- *So that the reader [does what? Thinks what?]*
- *So that next time we think about our family, we …*

Structure:
A possible structure for your answer: 'The writer communicates his feelings about going home through the use of ____________.' (Name your technique, provide your evidence, explain the effect, link back to purpose. Repeat this for a second and then a third technique.)

ISBN: 9780170424547

POETRY 3

Now that you have worked through two poetry texts, we will be starting to remove some of the activities. This doesn't mean that they are no longer important, but, rather, we are hoping that you are starting to work through them naturally yourself as you read the text. Remember to pay attention to the language used, the title, and your first impressions.

Reading the poem

1 Read the poem through once, slowly (out loud if you can). Don't do anything else; just read.

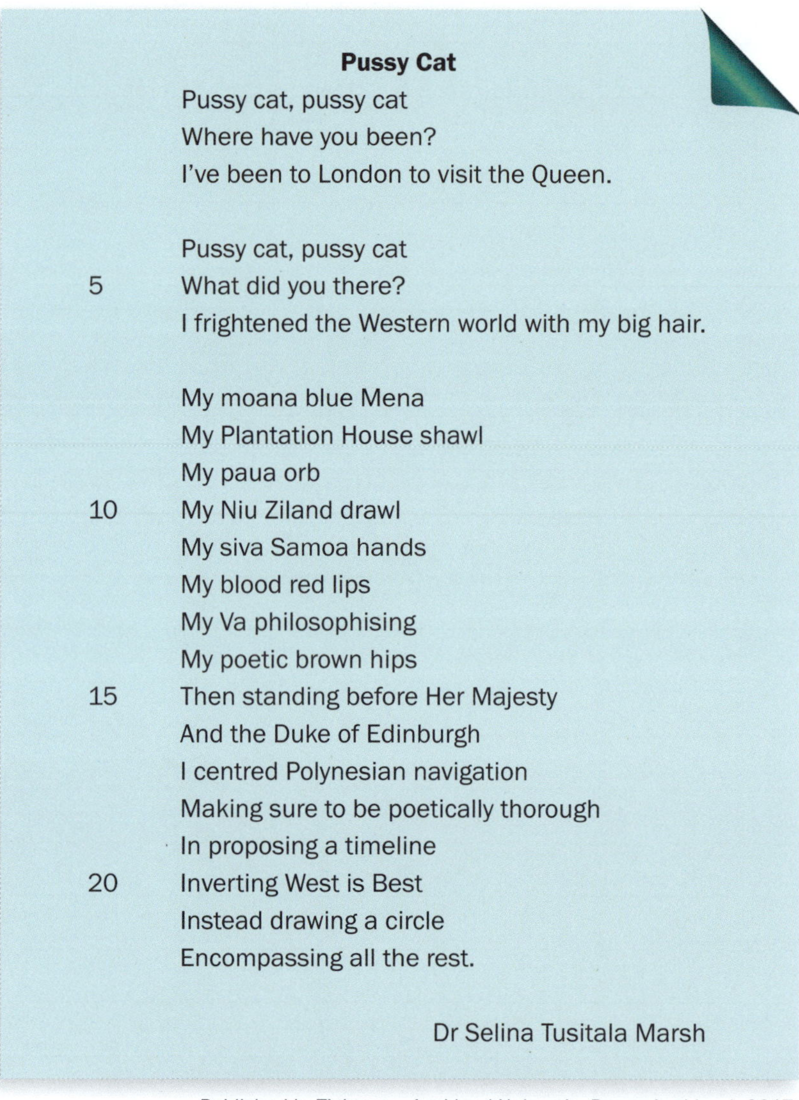

Pussy Cat

Pussy cat, pussy cat
Where have you been?
I've been to London to visit the Queen.

Pussy cat, pussy cat
What did you there?
I frightened the Western world with my big hair.

My moana blue Mena
My Plantation House shawl
My paua orb
My Niu Ziland drawl
My siva Samoa hands
My blood red lips
My Va philosophising
My poetic brown hips
Then standing before Her Majesty
And the Duke of Edinburgh
I centred Polynesian navigation
Making sure to be poetically thorough
In proposing a timeline
Inverting West is Best
Instead drawing a circle
Encompassing all the rest.

Dr Selina Tusitala Marsh

Published in *Tightrope*, Auckland University Press, Auckland, 2017.

G

Mena – a family-owned, contemporary fashion brand that reflects the pride in Samoan heritage
siva – dance
Va – this consists of relationships between people and things, unspoken expectations and obligations

About this poem

Dr Selina Tusitala Marsh is a Pasifika poet-scholar and New Zealand Poet Laureate (2017–19). She was commissioned to write a poem for the Queen of England and present it at Westminster Abbey. She recited it for Her Majesty at the Commonwealth Day Observance on 14 March 2016. The title of the poem is 'Unity'.

2 Record your first impressions of the poem below. You can write in bullet points, draw some images or write in full sentences.

3 **VOCABULARY WORK**

Read the poem again.

a Circle or highlight any words in the poem you are unfamiliar with.

b Use a dictionary or device to find the definition of your words (from task **a**) that make sense for this poem. Write that definition in the space provided.

Word 1: ____________________

____

Word 2: ____________________

____

Word 3: ____________________

____

Unpacking the text

1 Read the poem again. Pull out words that have negative and positive connotations (feelings and images we associate with them, rather than the literal meaning) and place them in the grid below.

Positive	Negative

2 Looking at your answers from above, what do you think is the overall **tone** of this poem and why? Give a quote from the poem to back up your opinion.

I think the tone of 'Pussy Cat' is negative/positive (delete one). I see this in the poem when it says '____________________

____________________'. This makes the tone ____________________ because ____________________

____

____________________.

ISBN: 9780170424547

Identifying how the poem is communicated

We have deliberately waited until near the end of your analysis to get you to identify techniques. This is because at Level 2 it is crucial that you **understand the ideas** in the poem in detail prior to understanding **how** they are communicated.

Fill in the following grid about the ideas in the poems and what **techniques** help communicate these ideas – we have started it off for you.

Technique	Evidence	Effect	Purpose
listing	moana blue Mena ... Plantation House shawl ... paua orb ...	Overwhelms the reader of all the things the poet believes frightened the 'Western world'.	To emphasise how many things the poet believes the West thinks is scary about being Polynesian.
metaphor	I centred Polynesian navigation drawing a circle	Describes the way the poet rearranged the telling of the historical accounts to be at the centre of the world view. Describes how the message she is conveying is like the physical act of putting a ring around the world.	
question	Where have you been? What did you there?		
alliteration	**W**estern/**W**orld/**w**ith **s**iva/**S**amoa/hand**s**		
repetition	My Pussy cat		
allusion	Pussy cat, pussy cat/ Where have you been?	Reminds us of the nursery rhyme.	
rhyme	there ... hair lips ... hips West ... Best ... rest		

Putting it together

ANALYSE

This means discussing **WHAT? HOW? WHY?** and **SO WHAT** (are we to do/think as a result)?

Annotate the question to remind yourself to address each aspect in your answer. Refer to the annotated question on page 40 if you need help.

Analyse how the writer both criticises and encourages the West in her poem.

QUESTION

Analyse how the writer both criticises and encourages the West in her poem.

In your answer you should include examples of techniques used in the text, and explain their effects. (These might include, but are not limited to: listing, metaphor, repetition, alliteration.)

You should start your answer using the words of the question.
If you are stuck, you can use some of the starter sentences below to help you.

- *The poet firstly criticises the West when she says ...*
- *What she means is ...*
- *The use of [technique] when she says [detail] is effective because ...*
- *The reader is challenged to think ... because ...*
- *Another way she criticises the West is by the use of [technique] when she writes [detail].*
- *The meaning of this is ... and relates to ...*
- *However, the poet also encourages the West to ... when she says ...*
- *The use of [technique] when she means ...*
- *The use of [technique] when she says [detail] is effective because ...*
- *The reader is challenged to think ... because ...*
- *Another way she encourages the West is by the use of [technique] when she writes [detail].*
- *The meaning of this is ... and relates to ...*
- *The purpose of this poem is to ...*

ISBN: 9780170424547

POETRY 4

This is the final text in this section with some activities. Try to remember all of the strategies you have learned so far, even if they have been left out in this series of activities. In the exam you will have no activities and will rely on your memory to help you use the different strategies. It is good to start practising now.

Reading the poem

1 Read the poem through once, slowly (out loud if you can). Don't do anything else, just read.

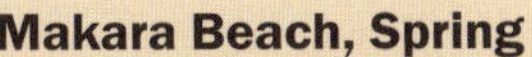

Makara Beach, Spring

It's this skin of happiness that holds
me together. Like an olive round an anchovy's
body. More loosely, like Maggie's neck
collected in folds over her collar bone
sliding about, no special grip on the world.
A dog's life all right. But god, it's good, beside
the sea collecting wild flowers and weeds
of new zealand. Blue eye daisies, white as foam
and dark as the sea's centre, the middle's
what counts, and yellow, there's yellow
flora all over the place. I've even got you
collecting the encroaching cream off
the land, and a smudge of silver edged
leaf. A heron
bows, arches, stalks across
stones. A bunch of overland cyclists stand
aside, smile. Indians picnic in the shade
of a cliff. A Vietnamese child lies down
waiting to be rescued on the round
rocks. A tide of gorse
flows over the hills flushed at the seams
with orange bloom. We agree to share botulism
if the crayfish roll at the tearooms
should fail us. Well yes. This is certainly
short enough to be happiness.
The morning's a ball
of silk unwound about us. You gather
it back with me at its centre.

Fiona Kidman

Essential New Zealand Poems, Godwit, 2014.

G

anchovy – a small herring-like fish found in the Mediterranean Sea
botulism – a sometimes fatal disease caused by spoiled foods (food poisoning)
heron – a long-legged, long-necked bird

ISBN: 9780170424547

2 Read the poem through again. This time, underline all of the words that have negative connotations.

3 With a different colour, underline all of the words with positive connotations.

4 What is the overall **tone** of the poem? ______________________ (Refer to the table on page 44 for suggestions if you need help.)

Linking the title with the end of the poem

1 Write down the title and the last two sentences of the poem.

2 What might the information above tell you about the poet's attitude towards life?

Identifying the 'point of change'

Identifying and understanding the point of change is a **key to analysing the poem**.

1 Identify the point of change in the poem according to the line number(s). __________

2 What is the poet trying to tell us by this point of change?

Identifying the poem is communicated

We have deliberately waited until near the end of your analysis to get you to identify techniques. This is because at Level 2 it is crucial that you **understand the ideas** in the poem in detail prior to understanding **how** they are communicated.

Complete the following grid of **language features**. We have started it off for you.

Technique	Example(s)	Effect
	me her I've you we	Helps us feel like we are at the beach with the poet, that we are experiencing these things alongside her. Because this is a poem set in New Zealand, we can easily imagine these scenes from our own memories and experiences.
	... skin of happiness ... Like an olive round an anchovy's body. ... like Maggie's neck ... ... white as foam ... ... dark as the sea's centre ...	
repetition		
parallel structure	A heron ... A bunch ... A Vietnamese child ... A tide of gorse	

ISBN: 9780170424547

Putting it together

ANALYSE

This means discussing **WHAT? HOW? WHY?** and **SO WHAT** (are we to do/think as a result)?

Annotate the question to remind yourself to address each aspect in your answer. Refer to the annotated question on page 40 if you need help.

Analyse how the writer uses the setting of Makara Beach as a way to communicate her view of New Zealand's society.

QUESTION

Analyse how the writer uses the setting of Makara Beach as a way to communicate her view of New Zealand's society.

In your answer you should include examples of techniques used in the text, and explain their effects. (These might include, but are not limited to: imagery, simile, repetition, parallel structure.)

If you are stuck, look back over the sentence starters provided earlier in this book.

ISBN: 9780170424547

POETRY 5

Now that you have completed the first four poetry text activities, you are ready to attempt a piece as if you were under exam conditions.

Using all the strategies you have been practising throughout this chapter, give this your best shot. Put your timer on for 20 minutes. Read the poem and use your strategies to answer the question. Good luck!

In this poem, the poet speaks directly to an ex-lover about how to manage now the relationship is over.

Advice to a Discarded Lover

Think, now: if you have found a dead bird,
Not only dead, not only fallen,
But full of maggots: what do you feel –
More pity or more revulsion?

Pity is for the moment of death,
And the moments after. It changes
When decay comes, with the creeping stench
And the wriggling, munching scavengers.

Returning later, though, you will see
A shape of clean bone, a few feathers,
An inoffensive symbol of what
Once lived. Nothing to make you shudder.

It is clear then. But perhaps you find
The analogy I have chosen
For our dead affair rather gruesome –
Too unpleasant a comparison.

It is not accidental. In you
I see maggots close to the surface.
You are eaten up by self-pity,
Crawling with unlovable pathos.

If I were to touch you I should feel
Against my fingers fat, moist worm-skin.
Do not ask me for charity now:
Go away until your bones are clean.

Fleur Adcock

Selected Poems, Oxford University Press, 1983.

ISBN: 9780170424547

QUESTION

Analyse how the writer's advice to her discarded lover reveals the nature of their relationship.

In your answer, you should include examples of techniques used in the text and explain their effects. (These might include, but are not limited to: imperative, personal pronouns, extended metaphor.)

ISBN: 9780170424547

POETRY 6

Using all the skills you have been practising throughout this chapter, give this your best shot. Put your timer on for 20 minutes. Read the poem and use your strategies to answer the question. Good luck!

And if it snowed

And if it snowed and snow covered the drive
he took a spade and tossed it to one side.
And always tucked his daughter up at night.
And slippered her the one time that she lied.

And every week he tipped up half his wage.
And what he didn't spend each week he saved.
And praised his wife for every meal she made.
And once, for laughing, punched her in the face.

And for his mum he hired a private nurse.
And every Sunday taxied her to church.
And he blubbed when she went from bad to worse.
And twice he lifted ten quid from her purse.

Here's how they rated him when they looked back;
sometimes he did this, sometimes he did that.

Simon Armitage

Poetry Diary 2013, Faber and Faber, 2012.

QUESTION

Analyse how the writer shows the different characteristics of the man in the poem.

In your answer you should include examples of techniques used in the text, and explain their effects. (These might include, but are not limited to: repetition, personal pronouns, contrast, adjectives.)

ISBN: 9780170424547

Section Three: NON-FICTION

A good thing about analysing a piece of unfamiliar **non-fiction** is that, because the writing is usually more explicit, the topic and purpose are much more obvious to the reader: the author wants to teach you something or persuade you to agree with them or motivate you to action about an idea. Oftentimes, it is all of these. Being successful in achieving the purpose matters to the writer.

In this chapter, we are going to specifically look at:

- **the what** (the subject matter or topic)
- **the how** (what language techniques are used and the effect of using these)
- **the why** (the writer's purpose and attitude towards the topic they are writing/speaking about)
- **the 'call to action'** (identifying the intended response of the reader and why).

'When you write non-fiction, you sit down at your desk with a pile of notebooks, newspaper clippings, and books and you research and put a book together the way you would a jigsaw puzzle.'

Janine di Giovanni

NON-FICTION 1

Pre-reading activities

Before you read the text, let's prepare by looking at some words that might be new to you. Next, we will look at ways to 'predict' the subject and purpose of a text.

1 VOCABULARY WORK

Look up the meaning of the following words and write the most common meaning beside it.

a furore ______________________________

____

b rehash ______________________________

____

c charity ______________________________

____

d paradigm ______________________________

____

e agency ______________________________

____

f by-products ______________________________

____

g prohibitive ______________________________

____

h demeaning ______________________________

____

i dispense ______________________________

____

j ostensibly ______________________________

____

k communist ______________________________

____

l disempowering ______________________________

____

m parental ______________________________

____

2 After considering these definitions, what do you think might be the subject matter of the text?

I think the piece will be about ______________________________

because ______________________________

____

______________________________.

The magic 'because'
The word 'because' is a magic word as it forces us to explain and justify our statements.

3 **THE TITLE**

The title of our first non-fiction text is 'We don't need our community to be grateful, we need them to be okay'.

a Write down what the idea of 'community' means to you.

____

____

b Write down what the idea of 'to be okay' means to you.

____

____

c What ideas do you think this piece might include?

____

____

d Write your prediction.

I think the piece will be about ______________________________

because ______________________________

____

____

4 THE BACKGROUND/CONTEXT OF THE TEXT

When you read a text, it is important that you take into consideration all the available information: who the author is, when the text was written, where the text is based, and any other details provided, as this can go some way to assisting you in understanding the purpose of the text and/or the point of view of the writer. In the exam, this information is usually provided at the heading of the piece, within the question, or in the small print under the text.

G

Abridged: (of a book, film, poem, etc.) shortened without losing the main sense of it.

The writer of this article is the spokesperson for a group that calls itself The Aunties. The group provides clothing, food and support for distressed women and their children who have just arrived at a Women's Refuge Centre. The article has been slightly edited and abridged.

a What things would you expect to be of concern to a person who works with the vulnerable?

____

____

b Thinking about the title and your predictions above, what do you think might be the main purpose of the article?

I think the piece will be about ______________________________

because ______________________________

____

____

Reading the text

1 Read the non-fiction piece through once, slowly (out loud if you can). Don't do anything else; just read.

We don't need our community to be grateful, we need them to be okay

I started a bit of a furore. You may have seen it mentioned on telly, on the radio, in the papers, or on social media before Xmas last year. All about tinned tomatoes. I won't rehash it here, but the thing is: it was never about tinned tomatoes. It was really about being a charity and being brave enough to say: this is what we need from you.

It was about trusting that people know what they want and need and providing access to those resources for them, so that they get to make their own choices. And the main point was this: the person who drives the resourcing should be the person who needs the support, and not the people giving it.

So how do we change the paradigm? How do we start looking at giving people agency? Let's start with the language. Language is incredibly important because the 'wrong' language can make people feel even more 'less than' they may already feel. More judged. More of a failure.

I've been around this stuff for a while now, and I've always used the words 'living in poverty' but recently, I've started using the term 'deliberately under-resourced'. Because that is, in my opinion, what it is. All the other words/terms are simply by-products of that under-resourcing.

A low wage economy, prohibitive rents, benefits that are set to be deliberately unlivable, and prohibitively high food costs.

We can also shift the paradigm by thinking about what charity actually means. It doesn't describe what the Aunties do, and it's demeaning to the people we support, and resource. We don't dispense charity – we are a whānau, a community, supporting and resourcing other members of our whānau. I've always said people need stuff, we get it for them. But it's a bit more complicated than that. Because you have stuff other people need, you get it to me, and ostensibly I give it to them, who need it, right? Kind of. What actually happens is that you offer me stuff, and I decide who can use it because I have a relationship with them, or their social worker, and in the cases where I know the person directly, I ask them. Or the stuff gets to the storage unit, and I don't even ask them what they need any more. I just tell them what's there, they come and get what they need or want. There's no middle person, it's just them making their own decisions.

Because we're not in 1960s communist Russia, right? When you go to the supermarket you take what you need, don't you? And there's a whole range of choices. The way I work things is that the stuff is there, all sorts of stuff, and you do the same thing. Except it's free. A number of charities have started doing this with food – they call it the food pantry approach. And I think that we need to move away from this model of charity where you get what you're given. It's disempowering and designed to make the person receiving feel awful. Because you have to be grateful. (We may leave that for another time, the idea of gratitude ...)

I've always said: give with love. I want to change that up. Gift with love. Resource with intent, and in a specific and client-based – hate the word, it'll do for the moment – way. Bring the focus back to the person who's getting what they need, and not the person who's giving it. Because, and here's something else to think about, there is a huge power imbalance in all of this. You have something they need, they feel the pressure to be grateful. Power imbalance.

We can move from a model of charity where we act as parental, to a model where we act as equals, as much as is possible. Empower people to do whatever they need to do to bring them out of those struggles, if that's what they want to do.

Because, we don't need our community to be grateful. We just need our community to be okay. All of us. To be okay. We can do that.

Jackie Clark

Accessed 3 April 2018 and abridged from: https://www.stuff.co.nz/auckland/local-news/manukau-courier/102581639/jackie-clark-we-dont-need-our-community-to-be-grateful-we-need-them-to-be-okay

2 What are your first impressions?

____

____

____

____

3 Read the text through again.

Think: what does the writer want us to think about/do/join/change, etc.? Write down one thing we are being encouraged to do as a result of reading this message.

The writer wants us to:

____

____

____

____

______________________________.

ISBN: 9780170424547

Unpacking the text

In a non-fiction text, whether it be an opinion piece, a persuasive piece or a speech, every paragraph contains an idea that relates to the overall purpose. This purpose is what the writer wants the reader to do or realise; our **call to action**. Think of the text as a jigsaw, in that each paragraph is a piece that connects to the pieces that come before and after. Looking at the individual pieces is what we call **unpacking the text**.

1 FIND THE PATTERN

In this task, we want you to look at each paragraph by itself and summarise the idea – the jigsaw piece – in one sentence. A couple have been done for you as an example.

1	The writer acknowledges she has created some controversy with her comments about charity.
2	
3	
4	
5	
6	
7	We need to move away from the old way of thinking about how to help people because that way makes people in need feel powerless.
8	
9	
10	

It is okay if you repeat similar things, as this is often the case because the author is repeating their idea in different ways to hammer home their point.

2 SUMMARISE

a In no more than three sentences, write what this piece is about.

b Complete the following sentence.

The writer wanted to teach us about ____

because ____

____

____.

Identifying the 'call to action'

Writers put their ideas out into the world because they want something from their readers: to change a belief, to understand a new concept or to get involved in doing something. This is a '**call to action**'. There are also ideas which relate to us regardless of who we are, where we are and what we do. These are called '**universal truths**'. If you can link this call to action to a universal truth during your analysis, then you will show that you have gained a richer/deeper understanding of the writer's purpose.

1 Look at the grid below containing a selection of messages from Clark's piece and a selection of possible actions the reader could take.

A: The universal truths according to the text	B: Our 'call to action'
There are enough resources for everyone but those in power seem to keep the poor in need.	Share what we have or challenge policy makers who are trusted with the responsibility of helping the vulnerable.
Everyone is different and people usually know what they need.	Trust their judgements and listen to them.
You can't ever understand a person until you have walked in their shoes.	Do not judge but rather take the time to get to know someone who is different to us.
Just because someone asks for help does not mean they are less of a person.	Don't be mean to them. Instead, see what we can do to help them.
He aha te mea nui o te ao? He tāngata, he tāngata, he tāngata. What is the most important thing in the world? It is people, it is people, it is people.	Understand that all lives are valuable and treat all people with respect and dignity.
Sometimes bad things happen to good people.	Change our attitude towards people who are struggling with poverty by asking what we can do to help.

2 Circle ONE of the 'universal truths' from list A.

3 Find an example from the text which shows this 'truth'.

____

____

____

4 Explain what the quote/example means.

____

____

____

____

5 Circle the corresponding 'Call to action' statement from list B.

ISBN: 9780170424547

6 **Extra for experts**: See if you can finish your paragraph with a 'therefore/so that' statement. We have done the first one for you as an example.

> According to this text, **there are enough resources for everyone but those in power seem to keep the poor in need.** We see this in the text when the writer says **'I've started using the term 'deliberately under-resourced'**. This means that she believes there has been a conscious decision by politicians to provide less of what is needed to those who are poor. So, the writer wants **us to share what we have or challenge policy makers who are trusted with the responsibility of helping the vulnerable** so that **we can all solve the problem**.

Your turn:

According to this text, ____

____. We see this in the text when the writer says '____

____'.

This means ____

____. So, the writer wants us to ____

____ so that we can

____.

Identifying how the idea is communicated

We have deliberately waited until near the end of your analysis to get you to identify techniques. This is because at Level 2 it is crucial that you **understand the ideas** in the text in detail prior to understanding **how** they are communicated.

Ideas are communicated through a variety of language features or language techniques for at least one of the following purposes:

- to include the reader
- to emphasise a point
- to highlight words or ideas
- to create a picture in the reader's mind (imagery)
- to challenge our thinking
- to encourage us to act (call to action).

Identifying the **pattern** and **call to action** of the text like you did in the earlier activities helps you understand the writer's purpose. This purpose is then communicated through a variety of **language features** or **language techniques**. These terms are used interchangeably in this book.

We have found these language features in this text. As you can see, there are a lot.

personal pronoun	imperative/command	listing	proper noun
parenthesis	adjective	parallel structure	use of te reo Māori
repetition	rhetorical question	anecdote	contrast
juxtaposition	short sentence	colloquial language	allusion
jargon	pun	alliteration	

Fill in the following grid – we have started it off for you.

Technique	Example(s)	Why it is effective	How does this develop our understanding of the writer's purpose?
personal pronoun	**I** started a bit of a furore. **You** may have seen **it** ...	She's writing about her experience but, because she wants to engage in a conversation, she includes the reader as well.	So that we feel this issue of how we treat people who need our help becomes personal to us.
repetition			
imperative			
colloquial language			
jargon			

ISBN: 9780170424547

Technique	Example(s)	Why it is effective	How does this develop our understanding of the writer's purpose?
listing			
short sentence			

 Putting it all together

Let's first take a moment to understand what the question is asking you to do.

ANALYSE

This means discussing **WHAT? HOW? WHY?** and **SO WHAT** (are we to do/think as a result)?

So, look at:

- Selection of detail (the what),
- Use of techniques (how). Look back to the language features you've identified. Which ones help you to understand the 'what'?
- The way words and images are structured (effect). This is where our earlier strategies will be helpful.

It is useful to annotate the question to remind yourself to address each aspect in your answer. We have done this for you this time:

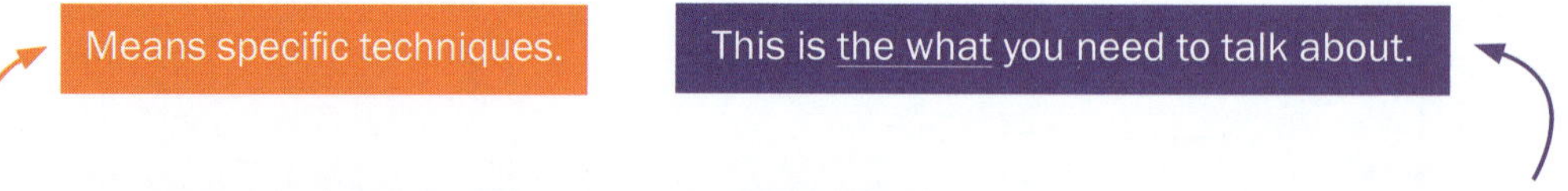

Analyse how the writer explains why society must change the way it helps those in need.

Means: What does the writer do?
- Selection of detail.
- Use of techniques.
- Way words/images are structured.

QUESTION

Analyse how the writer explains why society must change the way it helps those in need.

In your answer you should include examples of techniques used in the text, and explain their effects. (These might include, but are not limited to: repetition, personal pronouns, listing, imperative.)

Structure:
A possible structure for your answer: 'The writer explains why society must change the way it helps those in need through the use of ________________.'
(Name your technique, provide your evidence, explain the effect, link back to purpose. Repeat this for a second and then a third technique.)

You should start your answer using the words of the question.
If you are stuck, you can use some of the starter sentences below to help you.

- *The writer explains why society must change the way it helps those in need because she ...*
- *One way we see this is by the use of [technique], for example ..., which is effective because [explain the effect of the technique], as it helps us understand ...*
- *Another way the writer explains why society must change is by the use of [insert technique] and the use of [insert technique] when she writes [insert example] and [insert example].*
- *These techniques together emphasise the idea of [describe a message] because [describe effect of the techniques].*
- *Jackie Clark wants the reader to consider/think about/understand the idea or message [you could put in a 'universal truth'] because she wants us to [describe what action she wants from the reader], so that ...*

ISBN: 9780170424547

NON-FICTION 2

Pre-reading activities

Before you read the text, let's prepare by looking at some words that might be new to you.

1 VOCABULARY WORK

Create a sentence with each of these words in it (their definitions are given in brackets).

a CHOGM (Commonwealth Heads of Government Meeting)

____

b winkle-picker (a style of shoe or boot worn from the 1950s onwards, with a sharp and long pointed toe)

____

c abated (reduced in amount or degree; lessened)

____

d Allbirds (comfy sneaker-like shoes made from natural products)

____

e kahu huruhuru cloak (feather cloak)

____

f foray (a quick sudden attack)

____

g coup (a highly successful, unexpected stroke, act, or move; a clever action or accomplishment)

____

h sashayed (glided or moved easily)

____

i tangible (capable of being touched; real or actual)

____

j encapsulated (summarised or condensed; placed in a capsule)

____

k woo (to seek the favour, affection or love of)

____

l swooning (in a state of rapture)

____

2 LOOKING AT THE OPENING LINE – THE HOOK

> 'I think if we're going to give the PM a score on her European trip and attendance at CHOGM, we'd have to score her very highly.'

a Do you think this is a good 'hook' for the opinion piece we are going to read? Give reasons and don't forget a magic 'because'.

____

____

____

b Do you think this piece is going to be in favour of the Prime Minister's trip or not? Give reasons based on the information you have so far.

3 THE BACKGROUND/CONTEXT OF THE EXTRACT

When you read a text, it is important that you take into consideration all the available information: who the author is, when the text was written, where the text is based, and any other details provided, as this can go some way to assisting you in understanding the purpose of the text. In the exam, this information is usually provided at the heading of the piece, within the question, or in the small print under the text.

'Assured, authentic Jacinda Ardern impresses overseas' is an opinion piece written by Kate Hawkesby. She is a columnist for the *New Zealand Herald* and also the host of a local radio show.

a What things would you expect to be of concern to a radio talkback host?

b Thinking about the title you have now been given, the vocabulary, and the first line of this text, what do you think the main purpose of this text might be?

ISBN: 9780170424547

Reading the text

1 Read the non-fiction piece through once, slowly (out loud if you can). Don't do anything else; just read.

Assured, authentic Jacinda Ardern impresses overseas

I think if we're going to give the PM a score on her European trip and attendance at CHOGM, we'd have to score her very highly.

I'd give her a 10 out of 10.

My initial concerns about her winkle-picker shoes being on display in Europe, the shoe fashion capital of the world, were quickly abated by the NZ fashion she managed to rep (which hopefully distracted from her shoes). If the Kiwi designers had been able to extend their dressing of her to include footwear, that would've been great, but I guess we should just be grateful she wasn't wearing her Allbirds.

She's received huge raps however for the kahu huruhuru cloak she so elegantly wore to dinner with the Queen – she managed to pull that off in a way that seemed respectful and natural, as opposed to awkward or culturally inappropriate.

Ardern's authenticity has served her well. She's looked at ease, conversational and chatty with all leaders, and able to hold her own. You would not think this was her first foray onto this stage given the way she conducted herself.

It's also a coup to be able to look interested and enthused the entire time at what must have, at some points, been deadly dull. She pulled off what Camilla couldn't at the Commonwealth Games opening.

Double coup to do all of that while almost seven months pregnant – yes, I know it's not a disability or an illness, it's just a pregnancy, but it doesn't mean it's not tiring.

The other achievement for Ardern was seeming at ease and respectful around the royals. Notably, the Queen.

For a woman who believes we will see New Zealand become a republic in her lifetime, she sashayed through Buckingham Palace and conducted her toast at the state banquet like it was the most natural thing in the world. She even managed to publicly support Prince Charles as head of the Commonwealth.

The British and European press, though not really that interested in New Zealand's Prime Minister, did manage to say positive things when they did refer to her. That kind of coverage always makes Kiwis feel proud, and Jacinda herself will be pleased that after the ugly few weeks she'd endured here at home before she left, she's been able to impress on the world stage.

Nothing tangible comes out of CHOGM of course, well, not for a few years anyway, but the positive 'buzz' around it is all you can really hope for. She didn't trip up, embarrass us, say anything awkward, or wear her Allbirds in public view.

She encapsulated all the key ingredients to woo a swooning press: female, young, pregnant, smiley, upbeat, positive, culturally aware and considerate. Yes, it will be a great day when we have evolved enough to be able to take the words 'female, young and pregnant' off the list of notable aspects of her leadership.

But for now, these things are still a big deal. Ardern will be hoping now that the glow of this trip lasts at least another few weeks before she takes maternity leave to have her baby – after which the Jacindamania honeymoon, for the press anyway, will hit its revival once more. Mark my words.

Kate Hawkesby

Accessed 23 April 2018 from: http://www.nzherald.co.nz/nz/news/article.cfm?c_id=1&objectid=12037690

2 What are your first impressions?

3 Read the text through again. Think: what does Hawkesby want us to think about/do/join/change, etc.? Write down one thing we are being encouraged to do as a result of hearing this message:

Hawkesby wants us, as New Zealanders, to ______________________________

____

____

______________________________.

Unpacking the text

In a non-fiction text, whether it be an opinion piece, a persuasive piece or a speech, every paragraph contains an idea that relates to the overall purpose. This purpose is what the writer wants the reader to do or realise; our **call to action**. Think of the text as a jigsaw, in that each paragraph is a piece that connects to the pieces that come before and after. Looking at the individual pieces is what we call **unpacking the text**.

1 FIND THE PATTERN

In this task, we want you to look at each paragraph by itself and summarise the idea – the jigsaw piece – in one sentence. A few have been done for you as an example.

1	We have to give our PM a high score for her trip.
2	The author gives her top marks.
3	
4	
5	
6	She did better than the more experienced Camilla.
7	
8	
9	It's amazing she was at ease, as she doesn't believe in the monarchy.
10	
11	
12	
13	Ardern can enjoy this positive press for a while, and, when her baby arrives, it will start up again.

It is okay if you repeat similar things, as this is often the case because the author is repeating their idea in different ways to hammer home their point.

ISBN: 9780170424547

2 SUMMARISE

a In no more than three sentences, write what this piece is about.

____

____

____

____

____

____

____

____

____

b Complete the following sentence.

The writer wanted to teach us about ____

because ____

____

____.

Identifying the 'call to action'

Writers put their ideas out into the world because they want something from their readers: to change a belief, to understand a new concept or to get involved in doing something. This is a '**call to action**'. There are also ideas which relate to us regardless of who we are, where we are and what we do. These are called '**universal truths**'. If you can link this call to action to a universal truth during your analysis, then you will show that you have gained a richer/deeper understanding of the writer's purpose.

1 Look at the grid below containing a selection of messages from Hawkesby's piece and a selection of possible actions the reader could take.

A: The universal truths according to the text	B: Our 'call to action'
A person who is genuine can be trusted.	Always be true to ourselves.
Sometimes the polite thing to do is pretend to be interested even when you're not.	
You should always respect other people.	
We feel proud when someone from New Zealand does well on the international stage.	
Do not always believe what the media has to say.	
People are judgemental.	

2 Circle ONE of the 'universal truths' from list A.

3 Find an example from the text which shows this 'truth'.

____

____

____

____

4 Explain what the quote/example means.

____

____

____

____

____

5 Circle the corresponding 'Call to action' statement from list B.

6 **Extra for experts**: See if you can finish your paragraph with a 'therefore/so that' statement. We have done the first one for you as an example.

> According to this text, **a person who is genuine can be trusted**. We see this in the text when the writer says '**Ardern's authenticity has served her well**'. This means that Hawkesby believed that Ardern was herself at the CHOGM and that meant she represented New Zealand as a trustworthy country. So, the writer wants **us to always be true to ourselves and not pretend to be something that we're not** so that **others know they can rely on us**.

Your turn:

According to this text, ____

____. We see this in the

text when the writer says '____

____'.

This means ____

____. So, the writer wants

us to ____

____ so that we can

____.

ISBN: 9780170424547

Identifying how the idea is communicated

We have deliberately waited until near the end of your analysis to get you to identify techniques. This is because at Level 2 it is crucial that you **understand the ideas** in the text in detail prior to understanding **how** they are communicated.

Ideas are communicated through a variety of language features or language techniques for at least one of the following purposes:

- to include the reader
- to emphasise a point
- to highlight words or ideas
- to create a picture in the reader's mind (imagery)
- to challenge our thinking
- to encourage us to act (call to action).

Identifying the **pattern** and **call to action** of the text like you did in the earlier activities helps you understand the writer's purpose. This purpose is then communicated through a variety of **language features** or **language techniques**. These terms are used interchangeably in this book.

The following **language features** can be found in the text.

personal pronoun	imperative/command	listing
proper noun	use of te reo Māori	repetition
short sentence	colloquial language	jargon

Fill in the following grid – we have started it off for you.

Technique	Example(s)	Why it is effective	How does this develop our understanding of the writer's purpose?
personal pronoun	**I** think if **we're** going to give the PM a score ...	She's writing about her opinion but, because she wants to engage in a conversation, she includes the reader as well.	So that we feel that this idea of rating our Prime Minister is something that we are all a part of.
imperative/ command	Mark my words.		
listing			

Technique	Example(s)	Why it is effective	How does this develop our understanding of the writer's purpose?
proper noun			
jargon			
colloquial language			

Putting it all together

Let's first take a moment to understand what the question is asking you to do.

> **ANALYSE**
>
> This means discussing **WHAT? HOW? WHY?** and **SO WHAT** (are we to do/think as a result)?
>
> **So, look at:**
>
> - Selection of detail (the what),
> - Use of techniques (how). Look back to the language features you've identified. Which ones help you to understand the 'what'?
> - The way words and images are structured (effect). This is where our earlier strategies will be helpful.

It is useful to annotate the question to remind yourself to address each aspect in your answer. Fill in the blanks in the annotation. Refer to the annotated question on page 72 if you need help.

Means ______________________

This is the ______________ you need to talk about.

Analyse how the writer communicates her attitude towards Jacinda Ardern after her time at CHOGM.

Means: What does the writer do?

- ______________________
- ______________________
- ______________________

QUESTION

Analyse how the writer communicates her attitude towards Jacinda Ardern after CHOGM.

In your answer you should include examples of techniques used in the text, and explain their effects. (These might include, but are not limited to: personal pronouns, listing, imperative.)

You should start your answer using the words of the question. If you are stuck, you can use some of the starter sentences below to help you.

- *The writer's attitude towards Jacinda Ardern is one of ...*
- *One way we see this is by the use of [insert technique], for example [insert example], which is effective because [explain the effect of the technique], as it helps us understand ...*
- *Another way the writer communicates her attitude towards Ardern is through [insert technique] and the use of [insert technique] when she writes [insert example] and [insert example].*
- *These techniques together emphasise the idea of [describe a message] because [describe effect of the techniques].*
- *Kate Hawkesby wants the reader to consider/think about/understand the idea or message [you could put in a 'universal truth'] because she wants us to [describe what action she wants from the reader].*

Structure:
A possible structure for your answer:
'The writer explains why society must change the way it helps those in need through the use of ____________________.'
(Name your technique, provide your evidence, explain the effect, link back to purpose. Repeat this for a second and then a third technique.)

NON-FICTION 3

Now that you have worked through two non-fiction texts, we will be starting to remove some of the activities. This doesn't mean that they are no longer important, but, rather, we are hoping that you are starting to work through them naturally yourself as you read the text. Remember to pay attention to the language used, the background and your first impressions.

Reading the text

1 Read this transcript of a speech through once, slowly (out loud if you can). Don't do anything else; just read.

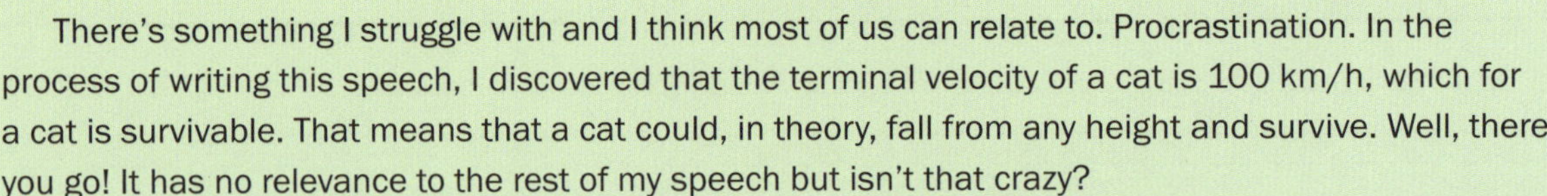

Procrastination

There's something I struggle with and I think most of us can relate to. Procrastination. In the process of writing this speech, I discovered that the terminal velocity of a cat is 100 km/h, which for a cat is survivable. That means that a cat could, in theory, fall from any height and survive. Well, there you go! It has no relevance to the rest of my speech but isn't that crazy?

Where was I? Oh yeah, that's right, procrastination. Procrastination: the act of delaying or postponing a particularly unpleasant or boring task. It can make our lives miserable! Many people say that the need to procrastinate comes from a deeply rooted desire for perfection and a fear of not reaching that. But if we're being honest with ourselves, there's a bit of laziness in there too. I am no stranger to the feeling of getting home from school all motivated and ready to tackle that essay head on. You sit down at your desk and remember that TV show you were watching yesterday. Just one episode won't hurt. Three hours later, you are ten episodes deep and have done zilch, zip, nada!

Social media. It's really addictive! Even if you're not the person to be constantly posting, you've got to admit, those cat videos on Facebook are addictive: cats are so much better than Maths revision; so is swiping down on Instagram and watching that little icon bring up a whole host of new pictures to look at instead doing one of the many, much more important things you could be doing.

Don't worry. It's not entirely your fault; social media is designed to leave us craving more. The swiping action to refresh a page had been engineered to act like the lever on a slot machine, meaning that social media companies are trying to get you as addicted to their app as some people are to gambling. And let me tell you, that is not good! Not good for your mental health and definitely not at all good for trying to actually do some work.

Completely removing all social media and internet communication is easier said than done and it would be a shame to completely lose the brilliant tool that has made communication so much easier. So instead, I challenge you to simply think about how much time you spend on social media or your phone in general and try to simply reduce. For example, something that works for me is: instead of checking your phone be the first thing you do when you wake up in the morning, hold off until you've achieved something. Anything! Start small, whether it's putting that pile of stuff away, or even something as simple as making your bed. Then challenge yourself! Keep pushing out how much you can do without picking up your phone or watching a YouTube video. It will help your day to start the right way, with pictures of other people's lives not being what sets the tone for your day. You'll also realise that getting stuff done feels great! Once you have that ball rolling from the beginning of the day, you'll find it so much easier to resist that temptation later when you're tired and the last thing you want to be doing is Maths. You'll know that you can do it and instead you'll get addicted to the feeling of finishing something and not having to worry about it ever again.

I'm going to leave you with something else I discovered while trying to write this speech. Get this! We each have 37.2 trillion cells in our body. Each cell has 2 metres of DNA, which means that you have 74.4 billion kilometres of DNA in your body! To put that into perspective, there is only 7.4 billion kilometres to get to Pluto.

So you are so complex that just the instructions needed to make you, can literally span the galaxy! That just proves that you are so much more than that little voice in your head saying 'just one more episode'. I dare you to defy those big social media companies: 'Not today. You're not stealing any more of my precious time.' Hide that phone! Close that tab! Just do it! Today I'm going to kick this essay's butt and tomorrow I'm going to change the world!

Annalyse Welford, Year 12, 2018.

Unpacking the text

1 FIND THE PATTERN

In this task, we want you to look at each paragraph by itself and summarise a key idea – the jigsaw piece – in one sentence. A few have been done for you as an example.

1	I struggle with procrastination.
2	
3	Social media is addictive and it's more interesting than doing homework.
4	
5	
6	You are a complex and valued organism and your time is worth protecting.

It is okay if you repeat similar things, as this is often the case because the author is repeating their idea in different ways to hammer home their point.

2 SUMMARISE

In no more than three sentences, write what this piece is about.

ISBN: 9780170424547

Identifying the 'call to action'

1 In the grid below, write down what you think might be universal truths and calls to action from Welford's piece. We have completed one for you.

A: The universal truths according to the text	B: Our 'call to action'
People will do almost anything to avoid painful or difficult work.	Recognise that it is normal to want to avoid hard tasks (procrastinate).

2 Choose one of the universal truths and its corresponding call to action from the grid above and complete the following.

According to this text, ____

____. We see this in the

text when the writer says '____

____'.

This means ____

____

____. So, the writer wants

us to ____

____

____ so that we can

____.

Identifying how the idea is communicated

We have deliberately waited until near the end of your analysis to get you to identify techniques.

Fill in the following grid about the ideas in the text and what language techniques help communicate these ideas – we have chosen some techniques and started filling in the grid for you.

Technique	Example(s)	Why it is effective	How does this develop our understanding of the writer's purpose?
personification	to kick this essay's butt	Helps us to imagine that the essay is something actively 'fighting' the speaker.	She wants to emphasise how hard she finds making herself sit down and write her essay, so by creating an image of the essay being something she is at war with, it helps us to understand the great effort she feels she needs to summon to finish her homework. Also, the phrase 'kick butt' is used to indicate that overcoming or winning *can* be achieve with the right attitude. You kick someone's butt when you are pushing them away from you and sending them on their way.
repetition	not good ... Not good ... not at all good		Because the speech is encouraging us to stop procrastinating, these commands are part of the solution to do that. Procrastination, according to the speaker, is about avoiding action. These imperatives command us to act, not just be passive listeners.
imperative			
personal pronoun			

ISBN: 9780170424547

Technique	Example(s)	Why it is effective	How does this develop our understanding of the writer's purpose?
colloquial language/ cliché			
short sentence		Sounds like somone snapping their fingers to get our attention.	
rhetorical question			

Putting it all together

ANALYSE

This means discussing **WHAT? HOW? WHY?** and **SO WHAT** (are we to do/think as a result)?

Annotate the question to remind yourself to address each aspect in your answer. Refer to the annotated question on page 72 if you need help.

Analyse how the speaker uses language features to communicate a serious message in an entertaining way.

QUESTION

Analyse how the speaker uses language features to communicate a serious message in an entertaining way.

In your answer you should include examples of techniques used in the text, and explain their effects. (These might include, but are not limited to: repetition, personal pronouns, facts/statistics, tone.)

You should start your answer using the words of the question.
If you are stuck, you can use some of the starter sentences below to help you.

- *According to this text the serious message the speaker wanted to get across ...*
- *One way we see this is by the use of [technique] for example [example] ...*
- *Which is effective because [explain the effect of the technique] it helps us understand ...*
- *We see this in the text when the writer says ...*
- *This means that ...*
- *So, the writer wants us to be ....*
- *These techniques together emphasise the idea of [describe a message] because [describe effect of the techniques ...*
- *The speaker wants to emphasise ...*
- *By creating an image of ...*
- *Also, the phrase ...*
- *Finally, the speaker wants us to consider ...*

ISBN: 9780170424547

ISBN: 9780170424547

NON-FICTION 4

This is the final text in this section with some activities. Try to remember all of the strategies you have learned so far, even if they have been left out in this series of activities. In the exam you will have no activities and will rely on your memory to help you use the different strategies. It is good to start practising that now.

Reading the text

Read the non-fiction piece through once, slowly (out loud if you can). Don't do anything else; just read.

The following is an abridged speech delivered by Maggie Rainey-Smith at an Anzac Day service.

I'm honoured to be invited to speak this morning on the centenary of the Gallipoli landings. I accepted this honour on behalf of my dad, a Second World War veteran who, when he was alive, marched here in Eastbourne, and today I wear his medals.

My father was a World War II veteran. He was also a small-town Kaikōura lad. I don't know, but I imagine he set sail with a sense of adventure on the *Aquitania* with the 22nd Battalion in May 1940. After a period in England and Egypt, he ended up in Greece with the 5th Field Regiment, led by Colonel Andrews, at Maleme, the strategic point where the battle for Crete was lost.

I've been to Maleme and walked around the cemetery, where thousands of the young German boys are buried – some as young as 16. It is sobering. I hadn't imagined that the German graves would move me more than the Kiwi graves at Suda Bay. Why? The sheer number of young German boys who were killed in the first two days of the battle is breathtaking.

On this same trip following my father's wartime experience, we travelled to Poland to visit Lamsdorf, the POW site on the Polish Czech border, to Stalag VIIIB, where my father spent four years of his life. I had expected to feel a huge sadness for my now deceased dad, but instead I found solace knowing that at least he was housed under the Geneva Convention in wooden huts along with other Commonwealth POWs – unlike the Russians who were left to perish, digging tunnels in the earth to find shelter.

Then there is the six hundred mile 'Death March' to consider. At the end of the war, the Germans knew the Russians and Americans were advancing and so they took their prisoners and marched them through sub-zero temperatures across Europe. Men who had survived four years or more as POWs succumbed and died on this march. My father watched as the man in front of him was shot dead for stopping to pick up a piece of bread which the locals had offered them. Local Germans who were also suffering and starving.

When my dad returned from the war he was diagnosed as having shell-shock, something that wasn't truly understood back then. For the rest of his life he suffered from anxiety and depression and regularly volunteered to undergo ECT treatment. I used to dread Anzac Day back then because of this, and yet I have indelible memories of it – my dad, his shiny brown shoes, his medals stitched lovingly to his suit by my mother, the military bands, the sense of occasion and the sense of community, the pageantry and afterwards the dreaded depression.

We lived with the aftermath of my father's war. I can't separate the man he might have been if he hadn't gone to war from the man he was. War is part of his story, and so it is part of mine. Anzac Day is a time when I feel connected to my community and to my family. In this the autumn of my own life, I celebrate the parades that link me to my dad, the whiff of boot polish, the drumbeats that stir me so, the haunting Last Post, the sausage rolls after at the RSA.

This morning as we recall the sacrifice of the Kiwis at Gallipoli, it is impossible as a mother not to mention the mothers and families of men and women involved in Iraq, Syria, Yemen, Gaza and the Ukraine to name just the high-profile conflicts.

I'd like to end with the words of Bertrand Russell: 'War does not determine who is right – only who is left.' Today I am here with my granddaughter proudly wearing my dad's medals on the right side. We are part of *who is left*.

ISBN: 9780170424547

Unpacking the text

1 FIND THE PATTERN

In this task, we want you to look at each paragraph by itself and summarise a key idea – the jigsaw piece – in one sentence. A few have been done for you as an example.

1	
2	My father was from Kaikōura and happily went off to fight in World War II.
3	
4	
5	The prisoners of war had to march 600 miles and many died.
6	
7	
8	
9	

It is okay if you repeat similar things, as this is often the case because the author is repeating their idea in different ways to hammer home their point.

2 SUMMARISE

In no more than three sentences, write what this piece is about.

Identifying the 'call to action'

1 In the grid below, write down what you think might be universal truths and calls to action from Rainey-Smith's piece. We have completed one for you.

A: The universal truths according to the text	B: Our 'call to action'
Everyone suffers because of war.	We must do all that we can to help not only the returning soldiers but their families as well.

2 Choose one of the universal truths and its corresponding call to action from the grid above and complete the following.

According to this text, ______________________________

______________________________. We see this in the

text when the writer says '______________________________

______________________________'.

This means ______________________________

______________________________. So, the writer wants

us to ______________________________

______________________________ so that we can

____

____

____

______________________________.

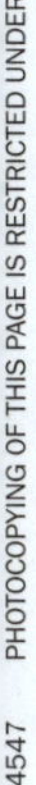

Identifying how the idea is communicated

We have deliberately waited until near the end of your analysis to get you to identify techniques.

Fill in the following grid about the ideas in the text and what language techniques help communicate these ideas – we have started it off for you.

Technique	Example(s)	Why it is effective	How does this develop our understanding of the writer's purpose?
personal pronoun	Today **I** am here with **my** granddaughter …	Makes it clear it is a personal account, which makes it more authentic because the writer is speaking from her experiences.	In recounting her experiences and explaining why she is here with her granddaughter, she is emphasising the ongoing effects of a soldier's choice to go to war – in this case her own father. It makes us think of our own family relationships, especially with those who have been affected by war.
pun		The play on words makes us appreciate the idea that there is often more than one response to a word or idea.	
alliteration			Emphasises the ideas of communities being connected by a shared experience: Anzac Day The hissing sound in the phrase mimics perhaps how someone in pain might feel. By making it the Germans (who were the enemy at that time), we can sympathise with them that they too suffered, not just our soldiers.
quotation	'War does not determine who is right — only who is left.'		
adjective		Provides a more specific image of the thing the speaker is talking about. They are strong adjectives.	
listing			By listing examples of things she remembers, the speaker reinforces the idea that, despite it being a long time ago now, such was the impact of war on her father (and her family), she still has very clear and specific memories of that time. This also enforces the idea that the 'end of the war' does not mean the end of its effects.

Putting it all together

ANALYSE

This means discussing **WHAT? HOW? WHY?** and **SO WHAT** (are we to do/think as a result)?

Annotate the question to remind yourself to address each aspect in your answer. Refer to the annotated question on page 72 if you need help.

Analyse how the speaker shows that, though war has terrible outcomes, she still believes Anzac Day should be commemorated.

Commemorate = to honour the memory of someone/something

G

QUESTION

Analyse how the speaker shows that, though war has terrible outcomes, she still believes Anzac Day should be commemorated.

In your answer you should include examples of techniques used in the text, and explain their effects. (These might include, but are not limited to: repetition, personal pronouns, contrast, adjectives.)

If you are stuck, look back over the sentence starters provided earlier in this book.

ISBN: 9780170424547

NON-FICTION 5

Now that you have completed the first four non-fiction text activities, you are ready to attempt a piece as if you were under exam conditions.

Using all the strategies you have been practising throughout this chapter, give this your best shot. Put your timer on for 20 minutes. Read the text and use your strategies to answer the question. Good luck!

This is the **abridged** introduction to the memoir ***Once While Travelling: The Lonely Planet Story*** by Tony and Maureen Wheeler. The Wheelers are the founders of the travel guide book company, The Lonely Planet.

Once While Travelling

Introduction

Lonely Planet began because people kept asking us, 'How did you get from Afghanistan to India? Not get sick? Hitch a ride on a yacht? ...' This book came into being for the same reason – people kept asking us, 'How did two backpackers with twenty-seven cents to their names end up running a multinational company?'

In much the same way as our initial journey sparked a great deal of interest in the minds of those people who dreamed of hitting the road, so the story of Lonely Planet seems to resonate with anyone who has dreamed of turning their passion into their work. Over the years we have given many interviews and public talks and we have often been asked the same questions: How much do we travel? How have we managed to remain business partners and married? How have we integrated our children into this lifestyle?

Lonely Planet has been on a journey for over thirty years and as it has evolved, so have we. We have grown from twenty-something backpackers with no money but a passion for travel to fifty-something owners of a multimillion-dollar company, still with the same passion.

Lonely Planet has been our life – we've lived it, breathed it and loved it – and while it hasn't always been easy or fun, it has never been boring. We've learned many lessons about business, about working and living together, about taking risks, working hard and what can happen if you throw yourself at the world with open arms and a lot of curiosity, so our story encompasses all of that: travel, work and relationships.

Tony and I continue to travel. We still believe it is important to encourage others to go and see the world and we continue to love what we do. Of course, we could not have done it without all those travellers who've put their trust in all of us at Lonely Planet. For every person who has used and abused our books, sent us letters from the road and thrown one of our guides into their bag as they set out on an adventure, thank you.

Maureen Wheeler

Abridged from *Once While Travelling: The Lonely Planet Story*, Viking, 2005.

QUESTION

Analyse how the writer communicates her views of why the book about the company Lonely Planet is worth reading.

In your answer you should include examples of techniques used in the text and explain their effects. (These might include, but are not limited to: personal pronoun, word choice, listing.)

NON-FICTION 6

Using all the strategies you have been practising throughout this chapter, give this your best shot. Put your timer on for 20 minutes. Read the text and use your strategies to answer the question. Good luck!

This extract is from an introduction to a collection of short stories by New Zealand women writers on their friendships.

Tessa: Some Thoughts on Friendship

Women have all the luck. Not only do we live longer, have babies, and get the choice of wearing the pants or a dress; in one of nature's lopsided lapses we also hold the main supply of intimacy. So, when a man needs support or solace, he'll generally turn to his all-purpose partner, or perhaps a sister or a woman friend, and that's about as much as he can expect. On the other hand, a woman, whether or not she has a mate, can call on three or four girlfriends, who are usually at the centre of a wider circle of female acquaintances, all eager to listen, talk, and – perhaps this is the bit that men miss out on more than anything – laugh about it.

Nor do we go without those consuming waves of obsession, yearning, and fear of rejection that heighten sexual relationships. As the title of this anthology suggests, many of these stories are written from the viewpoint of the one who admires, who feels lucky or grateful, or who gets addicted to – all especially potent states when you're young. And yet the almost physical need for a friend doesn't diminish as you get older.

I found this out when I moved with my young children and (then) husband to California for two years. Suddenly I knew nobody: it was not a condition I had ever considered before. Scanning the crowds for a face showing some sign of affinity, I felt like a lonely heart looking for a lover. I despaired at finding a kindred spirit amongst the purple-taloned absentee mothers who cruised up in Range Rovers to collect blank-faced Camerons and Tylers at the school gates.

Then one afternoon I spotted a dark-haired woman calling to her children in the playground. She was my type – I could tell from her clothes, her voice, her manner – so I made the move and started talking to her. Within minutes, we were laughing, sharing opinions and discovering things in common, including being new to the city. Soon we got to know her neighbour, a vibrant Jewish journalist from South Africa, and the three of us breathed a collective sigh of relief: we were fully alive again.

As the years pass, our friendships deepen. We cherish them more and maintain them more carefully. They are, as Fleur Adcock says here, 'more permanent, thank God, than marriage.' It was through a man that I first met Jane, and when he departed she befriended me. I remember helping her paint her kitchen, just days after the relationship had ended, my body still in shock. At the same time, I really wanted to do something for her, because her warmth and empathy with my grief were like balm. As we slapped off-white over the orange medallion wallpaper, she told me how she had once renovated her house after a particularly destructive break-up. 'The smell of paint,' she said in that direct, quotable way I would come to love, 'is the smell of loss.' For me, from that moment, it has always carried the whiff of hope.

It Looks Better on You: New Zealand Women Writers on their Friendships, edited by Jane Westaway and Tessa Copland, Longacre, 2003.

QUESTION

Analyse how the writer communicates her view that women's relationships are unique.

In your answer you should include examples of techniques used in the text, and explain their effects. (These might include, but are not limited to: listing, simile, sentence structure, word choice.)

GLOSSARY G

abridged (of a book, film, poem, etc.) shortened, without losing the main sense of it.

adjective a word that describes the noun. For example: hot, cold, blue, big, small.

adverb a word that describes the verb (how or when or where the action is done). For example: He smiled **sadly**. They were **nowhere**. **Yesterday**, I went to the park.

alliteration the repetition of consonant sounds. For example: **T**iny **T**im **t**ro**d** on **D**on's **t**oes. (The 'd' is also alliteration.)

allusion a reference to another literary or well-known work or person. For example: I was no Shakespeare but I loved writing plays.

anecdote a story used to illustrate an idea. For example: When I was a small child ...

assonance the deliberate repetition of the same vowel sound followed by a different consonant sound. For example: A st**i**tch **i**n t**i**me saves n**i**ne. The 'i' sound in 'stitch' and 'in' are the same; the 'i' sound in 'time' and 'nine' are the same.

attitude the opinion, point of view, type of behaviour of a person about a topic, person or thing.

book-ending phrases and/or ideas placed at the beginning and at the end of a passage.

cliché an over-used expression. For example: It was a dark and stormy night.

colloquialism informal language, usually spoken. For example: Howzit going, bro?

compound word two or more words are joined together to form a new word; sometimes joined with a hyphen (-). For example: babysitter, mother-in-law, homegrown.

conjunction a word that joins two sentences together. For example: and, but, so, because, therefore.

connotation something suggested or implied by an object or thing. For example: Black cats always make me nervous.

contrast the use of words or images that are opposite in likeness. For example: I was feeling hot and cold all night.

convincing including more than one example to support what you are saying and explain what you mean (magic 'because').

direct address when the narrator is speaking directly to the reader. For example: I'm interested in *your* thoughts on global warming.

euphemism a nicer way of saying something that is usually unpleasant or unkind. For example: He was 'let go' (fired). She's under the weather (sick).

extended metaphor a metaphor is used and then multiple comparisons are added to develop the image.

extract a passage or part taken from a book or article.

facts/statistics numbers and specific examples used to support an argument. For example: Around 65% of statistics are made up. She's worked here for 18 years so knows what is going on.

fiction made-up stories to entertain, persuade and/or teach a moral.

hyperbole an exaggeration. For example: I'm so tired I could sleep for a month.

imagery used to communicate visually an idea and/or create a mood.

imperative/command an order or command for an action. For example: Don't hit your sister.

incomplete sentence a sentence without a verb and or a subject. For example: Unfortunately for them. After the rain.

infer hint, imply, suggest.

jargon specialised language used by people who work together or share a common interest. For example: Getting **endorsement** for all **subjects** is good, but you still need to have **Level 2 Literacy** for **University Entrance**.

ISBN: 9780170424547

juxtaposition the deliberate placing of two things side by side by comparison or contrast. For example: We invited both our friends and our enemies.

listing related words or phrases arranged as a list. For example: I eat toast, cereal and a banana for breakfast.

literal strict meaning, true to fact, not exaggerated.

magic 'because' 'because' is a magic word, as it forces us to explain or justify our statements.

metaphor a comparison between two things where one thing is said to be another. For example: The playground **is a jungle**. All the students **are wild animals**.

narrator the person or character who is telling the version of events/story.

non-fiction a piece of writing based on facts and reality or offering an opinion. For example: biography, autobiography, textbook, letter to the editor, speech.

onomatopoeia the sound of the word imitates or suggests the meaning or noise of the action described. For example: crash, gurgle.

parallel construction/structure repeating the same word class order in close succession, e.g. proper noun + adjective + verb + preposition + noun. For example: 'It was the best of times; it was the worst of times' (*A Tale of Two Cities*, Charles Dickens).

perceptive making links between the ideas in the text and your observation of the wider contexts (either the fictional world of the text or the real world).

personal pronoun words that stand in place of proper nouns. For example: he, she, me, you, I, we, us, them, they.

personification when a non-living thing is given living characteristics or when a non-human thing is given human characteristics. For example: The lift groaned on the way down.

phrase a sequence of two or more words working together as a single image or idea. For example: a broken down rust heap.

preposition a word used to show the position of a thing in relation to another thing. For example: on, above, behind, inside, under.

pun an expression that plays on different meanings of the same word or phrase. For example: I've been to the dentist so many times, I know the drill.

quotation direct use of another's words, either spoken or written. For example: As the principal reminds us, 'To lead, you must serve.'

repetition words or statements used more than once for effect. For example: The room was cold. Too cold to think.

rhetorical question a question to which no answer is required. Used for dramatic effect. For example: Who knows?

rhyme the repetition of words with similar sounds. For example: There was an old horse from Cant**ucket**, who ate from a rusted brown b**ucket**.

rhythm the beat or pattern of stresses that occur in poetry and music and often used for effect in prose.

short sentences one- to three-word sentences, often phrases. For example: Try it. Now.

show understanding explain your statements in terms of the meanings and effects created.

sibilance repetition of 's' sounds in two or more words; often used to indicate a sinister event or feeling. For example: The **s**lippery **s**nake **s**lithered acro**ss** the gra**ss**.

simile a phrase that compares two things, using 'like', 'as' or 'than'. For example: They behave **like** monkeys in the classroom, but are **as well behaved as** royalty in the playground.

stanza a grouping of lines in a poem similar to verses in a song.

symbol an image/picture that represents an idea. For example: A dove represents peace.

tone the overall impression of the author's attitude towards a topic, event or character. For example: humorous, sad, happy, peaceful.

use of punctuation the deliberate use of the comma or exclamation mark or ellipsis or other punctuation marks for effect.

use of te reo Māori using Māori words, expression — often without immediate translation. For example: Kia ora, friends, I send my aroha to you.

verb a doing word. For example: I **ate** my lunch, then **walked** to class.

ISBN: 9780170424547

ANSWERS

You will find some sample answers to the activities here. Many of the questions do not have one correct response so if you get a different answer to us, don't assume you are wrong. Think about why we wrote that answer and why you wrote your answer. Talk to someone else about their answer. Discussing how and why you came to a response is another Excellence skill to learning how to get familiar with unfamiliar texts. Most of the time in English analysis, provided you can support it with clear examples and explanations, your answer is correct for your reading of the text. We have written paragraph-type 'answers' for the final questions for each text. Some of the answers are short and some are much longer. This is because we felt that for some of the texts, there were many different examples that could be discussed in the answer. The phrases and sentences in **orange** indicate Merit-level commentary (convincing); the phrases and sentences in **blue** indicate Excellence-level responses (perceptive). To achieve at **Merit** or **Excellence** level, you are expected to provide a range of examples as you analyse how a text has communicated a specific idea.

NARRATIVE PROSE

NARRATIVE PROSE 1: 'Tending the Books' from *The Thirteenth Tale*

Pre-reading activities, page 8

Possible answers:

1

Word	Literal definition	Connotations
books	A series of pages assembled for easy reading	Stories, an activity where you can relax and lose yourself into a story
second-hand	Used (goods, etc.)	Not new; someone else used to own it; not as valuable
bookshop	A store where books are sold	Fun place filled with lots of books of all different kinds
dead/death	No longer alive/the end of the life of a person or organism	Grief, sadness, disappeared, no longer around

2 Caring for, looking after/looking after frequently or regularly.

3 Someone dies in a second-hand bookshop while taking care of someone who is looking to buy an old book.

Reading the text, page 9

2 Answers will vary.

Unpacking the text, pages 9–11

1 a i Positive: tend; happy; baluable; significant; laughter; humour; comfort; light; soul; feather; touch; hope; miracle, magic.
Negative: dead; dull; banal; disappeared; die; bones; ceases; dreadful; annihilation; corpses; graves; forgotten darkness; lonely.

ii and iii Answers will vary.

b i This extract is about books and the stories they contain, as well as what they mean to people. It explains how the character cares for the books in her bookstore and what they mean to her.

ii Possible answer: 'As one tends the graves of the dead, so I tend the books. I clean them, do minor repairs, keep them in good order.'

c The tone is mostly **positive** because of such words as **tend**, **happy**, **laughter**, **warmth**.

d The writer is **in awe of the power of something so simple** because she uses words like **'It is a kind of magic'** when discussing **the impact of reading words/thoughts from someone long dead all because these words were published in a book.**

2 a Paragraph 1: These books are not really all that important or valuable. They are often not very interesting either.
Paragraph 2: Words have the magic to cause us to feel emotions and capture the essence of the writer.
Paragraph 3: Tending books and the words of the dead is like tending graves.

ISBN: 9780170424547

b The writer wants us to understand that books are important because **they contain the ideas and thoughts and reflections of people who have lived before us** and that it's important that we understand this so that **we remember to keep reading so that we have our own lives enriched. I think she also wants to encourage those of us who like to write: to remember that what we say is valuable not just to us but to others, even strangers.**

Identifying how the text is communicated, pages 11–12

Technique	Example(s)	Why it is effective	How does this develop our understanding of the writer's purpose?
simile	like flies in amber like corpses frozen in ice	Paints an image of objects getting preserved physically so that you can relate that to mental ideas from books being preserved in writing.	She is wanting us to recognise how everlasting/ permanent people's words are, especially if they are printed in books. This preservation adds to the value of what is contained in the books but also shows how valuable are the people who wrote the words. Their words are like monuments that are erected publicly to honour famous/important people.
adjective	dreadful dead warmth real old	Gives us specific images for each of the nouns/ things mentioned.	Because the writer says that books help us to 'see' something that is frozen in time, the describing words allow us to appreciate more clearly how words made us understand why books and their (dead) authors are valuable to her – she wants us to see them in the same way she does.
rhetorical question	Do they sense it, these dead writers, when their books are read? Does a pinprick of light appear in their darkness? Is their soul stirred by the feather touch of another mind reading theirs?	To make you think whether this actually happens or not, whether this could possibly happen.	Since the writers essentially put a piece of their soul into their writing and if you believe in heaven, or a place where souls go after you die, then this could definitely be a possibility and therefore supports the idea of immortality when thinking about the value of books, their authors and being a writer in general.
listing	Their voice, their laughter, their warmth of their breath. Their flesh. Eventually their bones. Their humour, their tone of voice, their moods. They can comfort you. They can perplex you. They can alter you.	Provides a range of examples and details that are used to expand the understanding or description of what books can do for the reader.	Emphasises the effect that books can have on you as a person and what you can sense about the writer through their writing.

Putting it all together, pages 12–13

The writer describes her role as a worker in a second-hand bookshop in a positive way because she wants the reader to understand the value of books and the people who write them. She does this by listing a number of different effects that books can have on a reader when she says, 'They can comfort you. They can perplex you. They can alter you', which has the effect of providing a range of emotions experienced when reading books – **not always positive. The words 'comfort' suggest you might read when you are distressed whereas the word 'perplex' suggests the power of books to challenge our way of thinking. Ending the list with 'alter you' underlines that, no matter what effect, we are changed by reading. The writer recognises that just as books and their authors are different, readers may have a different response to reading. She lists these examples to ensure that all of our reactions are covered.**

The writer also uses a lot of adjectives because books help us to 'see' something that is frozen in time. The describing words such as 'dead', 'real', 'old', etc. allow us to appreciate more clearly how words made us understand why books and their (dead) authors are valuable to her – she wants us to see them in the same way she does. These adjectives give us specific images for each of the nouns/things mentioned.

Another way the writer shows this positive attitude to the role **and privilege** of being a second-hand bookshop worker is by the use of rhetorical questions like 'Is their soul stirred by the feather touch of another mind reading theirs?' and the use of simile, 'like corpses frozen in ice'. She is wanting us to recognise how everlasting/permanent people's words are, especially if they are printed in books. **This preservation adds to the value of what is contained in the books but also shows how valuable as well are the people who wrote the words.** These techniques together emphasise the idea the writer is hoping to communicate that deceased authors can feel when someone is reading and enjoying a book they wrote and, by asking us, we consider the possibility that this might be true. **We join the writer in her imaginations about the writers of these books so that she also is not 'alone' in her opinions and therefore this adds weight to the possibility to a 'yes' answer to her question. The writer thinks this because she believes it would be lonely being dead and she thinks that it would make the deceased authors happy to know that even once they are gone, their books and that little bit of their soul is still being appreciated.**

Setterfield wants the reader to understand that the books are something special to her because to her they are the remains of people who have died. **That they are little pieces of the author's soul, and that the author can feel how they are being treated and when they are being read. She is reminding us of the legacy you leave behind after death and how the written word is a great way to preserve your memory, thoughts and ideas for long after everything else you were is gone. Though being a worker in a second-hand (and by implication 'used' or 'not as valued') shop is seen as a lowly job, her use of effective imagery and vocabulary and pulling us into her musings elevate the status of the role to one who is a curator – like a museum that houses precious artefacts.**

ISBN: 9780170424547

NARRATIVE PROSE 2: We're Only Joking

Pre-reading activities, page 14

1 Possible answers:
   a human rights: fundamental rights, especially those believed to belong to an individual and in whose exercise a government may not interfere, as the rights to speak, associate, work, etc.
   b mainstream: the principal or dominant course, tendency, or trend.
   c plastered (plaster): smeared (a composition of lime, sand and water, allowed to harden and dry).
   d anecdote: a short account of a particular incident or event, especially of an interesting or amusing nature.

2 Possible answers:
   a

Word	Literal definition	Connotations
We're	We are We – more than one are – plural	We are in this together, we are going to do something, this will happen
Only	Solely, exclusively, without anything further	Not a big deal, short, won't take long, limited amount
Joking	Something said or done to provoke laughter, not to be taken seriously	Having a laugh, nothing to worry about, killing time

   b Answers will vary. All should be marked as correct as long as they refer back to the title or vocabulary words.

Unpacking the text, page 16

1 The subject of the story is Roger.
2 Any three of: 'He's dressed in trademark black, looking down at the ground.'; 'the slightly chubby boy'; 'wouldn't be any closer to being normal'; 'he calls out with a crazy smile'; 'plastic grin'
3 Negative (some suggestions): loan wolf; black; mushrooms; edge; chubby; Mars; fierce; argument; crazy; kill; explosions; roars; laughter; weird; betray; burying; mutter; broken; upset; pitiless; python
4 Positive (some suggestions): laughter; smile
5 Negative: there is a sense of guilt coming from the narrator about the way he ignored Roger and used him to get laughs from his friends.

Linking the title with the end of the text, page 16

1 We're Only Joking; Like a pitiless python, our laughter wrapped itself around Roger, its bright poisonous scales warning others away and squeezing him out of our lives.
2 Reading the title and the last line of the story together lets me know that the writer feels a sense of guilt towards the way he treated Roger. Even though he thought he and the other kids were only joking, what they didn't realise until too late was that their laughter at Roger made life unbearable for him and the only solution for him was to leave.

Identifying how the text is communicated, page 17

1 Extended metaphor: lone wolf, young wolf
   Imagery: heavy-duty headphones cover ears; army-style boots create mushrooms of dust
   Metaphor: a lone wolf, young wolf, mushrooms of dust
   Adjective: army-style, crazy, fierce, chubby, plastic
   Personification: mind is racing
   Rhetorical question: Wasn't he?, what harm can I do?
   Simile: Like a pitiless python, our laughter wrapped itself around him.
2 Lee compares Roger to a lone wolf. This is a significant comparison as it builds an image in our minds of a lonely, hungry and somewhat desperate wolf roaming the wilderness alone. It also makes us feel sad, as the wolf is a pack animal and therefore not meant to be alone. This metaphor is extended as Lee again compares Roger to a wolf towards the end of the story when he says he is a 'young wolf kicked out of his pack'.
3 Lee states that Roger was weird but then asks himself, and therefore the reader, 'Wasn't he?' This rhetorical question forces the reader to think about society's expectations and how people feel the need to fit in, and judge people that don't fit in. Soon after Lee asks a second rhetorical question, 'I'm only one person, what harm can I do?', which again forces the reader to think about experiences they have had in the their own lives and times when they might have made fun of those different from the mainstream. It makes us aware that all of our actions have consequences and that if others are acting the same way as us, it can add up to a watershed amount.

ISBN: 9780170424547

Putting it all together, pages 17–19

The writer is feeling guilty about his part in Roger's decision to leave school, and the purpose of this piece is to force us to reflect on our treatment of other people. Lee compares Roger to a wolf at the beginning and the end of the text. This extended metaphor brings an image to mind of a wild animal who shouldn't be alone, who should be part of a pack that works together to provide food and shelter for each other but, instead, Roger is 'a young wolf kicked out of his pack to roam the forest alone'. **This imagery makes it clear to us that Lee feels guilty. The use of the word 'kicked' has the connotations that Roger didn't have a choice in this, that he wanted to stay part of the pack (group) but the group decided to make him fend for himself.** We know that Roger is isolated at school through lines such as 'the slightly chubby boy might as well be on Mars' and part of Lee realises that his use of Roger as a humorous anecdote is 'only burying Roger deeper' but he doesn't really understand what harm he does as one person. When the news arrives that Roger has left school, Lee feels intensely guilty for a short time: 'Inside, a small part of me has broken. Not enough to make me feel upset for long, but enough to make me think.' **What Lee is thinking about is collective and individual responsibility.** Lots of people at school were unaccepting of Roger's differences and instead were mean to him. As Lee points out, all of these people would have been thinking, 'I'm only one person, what can I do?' but he drives his overall point home with the final line, which is the simile, 'Like a pitiless python, our laughter wrapped itself around Roger … warning others away … squeezing him out of our lives.' **Lee wants us to answer that rhetorical question and take responsibility for our own individual actions. We have no idea what other people are going through and how our (perceived) small action might be compounding with other people's actions, words and decisions towards that person (the collective impact).** Although there is no lasting impact for Lee from the meanness of his individual actions towards Roger, eventually this isolation from the school community caused by their collective behaviour made Roger leave. **It took this extreme event for Lee to reflect on his actions as an individual. Lee's message is to make us take a second thought before we say or do something that might hurt someone else. We can't control other people's behaviour but we can control our own.**

NARRATIVE PROSE 3: from *All We Shall Know*

Unpacking the text, page 21

1 The kite (object) is the subject of the text.
2 Any three of: 'the kite, pink and purple and shaped like a butterfly'; 'with long streamers of blue and gold'; 'danced left and right'; 'its streamers snaked around it'; 'hoisted its flimsy body'; 'snap the butterfly's spine across his knee'
3 Negative: breaking; downwards; suddenly; wet; For God's sake; shouted; flung; snaked; reddening; hoisted; flimsy; crashed; Oh, forget it; snap; broken
4 Positive: beach; sun; warm breeze; tide; barefoot; kite; smiling; lifted; skyward; pink; purple; butterfly; streamers; danced
5 Overall the tone is negative. Melody was happy and excited to fly the kite but it quickly turned to sadness.

Identifying the 'point of change', pages 21–22

1

First time	Second and third time
… he let the reel out quickly and smoothly, and the kite, pink and purple and shaped like a butterfly, with long streamers of blue and gold, danced left and right in a shifting wind before tumbling suddenly downwards …	… grabbed by some invisible hand and flung towards the ground … its streamers snaked around it … hoisted its flimsy body to the wind … it crashed again …

2 The tone has changed from a **positive** description of flying a kite to **seeing it in a negative way**. I think this is because **Melody's father is getting frustrated that he can't make it fly and he feels stupid in front of his wife and child. Melody is picking up on the tension between her parents.**
3 From this story, we can infer that the relationship between Melody's parents isn't great. She isn't sure if her mother is smiling when they are at the beach and then her mother quickly starts having a go at her father: 'For God's sake, Michael'. Her father keeps trying but he can't win. Melody feels stuck in between her parents: 'And I stood equidistant between them'.
4 The kite symbolises the failing relationship between Melody's parents. It has moments of hope, 'danced left and right in a shifting wind', but it is failing as it was once again 'grabbed by some invisible hand and flung towards the ground'. When Melody's mother leaves without saying goodbye, Melody sees her father 'snap the butterfly's spine across his knee and toss its broken body to the waves'. This symbolises that the relationship is over.
5 We can infer that Melody is 'in the middle' of her parents' unhappiness and that the impact of the situation is that she feels trapped and she is unsure how she should respond to the way they treat each other because she loves them equally. At that point, she was not on 'either side' but valued them both. The moment her mother takes her hand and pulls her away (changes the 'equidistance') is the moment she realises the depths of feeling she has for her father.

ISBN: 9780170424547

Identifying how the text is communicated, page 23

Some suggestions.

Technique	Example(s)	Why it is effective	How does this develop our understanding of the writer's purpose?
parallel structure	There was a day ... There was sun ... There was a spray ...	Helps build an image in the reader's mind to set the scene, creates a list of images that are all equally important.	Sets it in the past with the use of 'was' and also contrasts the images at the end of each phrase
personal pronoun	My I she he	Helps create a sense of belonging and immediacy.	Melody feels the same about both of her parents as she refers to them in a similar way (expect when she leaves her father with her mother, when she looks back she refers to him as 'Daddy')
simile	the kite ... shaped like a butterfly	Buttiflies are symols or beauty and freedom and hope. For a child, there is always a sense of wonder about a butterfly because it is so delicate and so beautiful.	Shows how harmless the kite is which contrasts with later in the piece when the kite has crashed. This description makes the negative more so because we see the beauty first.
adjective	pink, purple, blue, gold, dancing, wet, sand	Builds a very clear image in our minds of what Melody is seeing. It also helps us understand the tone as she starts off referring to everything in positive words and then changes to negative words as she picks up on her mother's negativity.	Melody's account of the day is affected by the words chosen to describe what is seen and heard. These adjectives reinforce her feelings of happiness and then of dispair when she is affected by her mother's unhappy mood.
repetition	forget it, forget it	Shows us the mother's frustation with the father and how she dismisses him.	The real thing she is saying is to forget the relationship because clearly he has been trying to make it work. Because the kite is the symbol for their marriage (and both become tangled) the mother, in her frustration, doesn't want to try to fix it – neither the kite nor the marriage.
long sentences/ lack of punctuation	And my father shouted ... snaked around it. (one sentence)	Ryan uses little punctuation in this extract. It makes it feel like we are standing with Melody and watching the events unfold as she is.	The dissolution of the relationship is a long-winded and painful one – tiring and hard to bear.
symbol	danced left and right ... hoisted its flimsy body to the wind ... snap the butterfly's spine across his knee	The kite is a symbol of her parent's failing relationship.	Children in distress often project their sadness and fears onto inanimate objects. Rather than confront the realty of what is happening, child Melody uses this kite to reflect what she is observing within her parent's marriage.

Putting it all together, pages 24–25

Melody's experience at the beach is one of growing awareness of the failure of her parents' marriage. The writer communicates this experience with the use of simile, repetition and symbolism. Initially, the kite is described as 'pink and purple and shaped like a butterfly'. The simile shows that the kite is a free, harmless and beautiful creature, just like the butterfly. **After the kite has crashed for the second time, Melody describes it as having 'its streamers snaked around it'. This change from describing it as a beautiful butterfly to a sinister snake shows Melody's growing awareness that the innocent family outing is loaded with tension.** The repetition in the text is used by Melody's mother, 'it'll fly, it'll fly' and 'forget it, forget it'. The effect of this repetition is that it emphasises and exaggerates the mother's impatience and frustration with her husband trying to fly the kite. The kite itself is a symbol of the relationship between Melody's parents. In the text, the father tries to fly the kite three times, and the mother gives him criticism on his technique/approach each time and gets more fed up and impatient as he tries; **we see this when she says to him, 'For God's sake, Michael'. Through the kite, the father shows how he is the one fighting for the relationship, as he keeps persisting to try to fly the kite even though it is being 'flung towards the ground' by an 'invisible hand'. Melody feels trapped between her parents, which is shown through the line 'I stood equidistant between them'. When her father fails the third time, her mother takes Melody's hand and leads her away from her father. It is only when Melody is taken away by her mother that her father finally gives up: 'I saw him snap the butterfly's spine across his knee and toss its broken body to the waves.' This shows how the kite symbolises the parents' relationship and when the father breaks the kite, he is finally giving up his hope on the relationship surviving. When Melody is led away from her father, she refers to him as 'Daddy' for the first time. The word 'Daddy' has positive connotations of love, closeness, support, fun and protection. This careful word choice and change from referring to him as 'her father', which is quite distant and cold, shows she realises just how much love and affection she feels towards him only when she is being taken away from him.** Overall, Melody's experience at the beach, which should have been an innocent family outing, is a negative one, as she is made aware of the failing of her parents' relationship.

ISBN: 9780170424547

NARRATIVE PROSE 4: from *Motueka Tobacco Farm, 1962*

Unpacking the text, page 27

1. The subject of the passage: Looking at the tobacco plantation in the valley.
2. Positive: laughed; reliable; gently; dreamer; music; laughter; love; song; smile; clearly; new; pleased; appealed; free; good; pleasurable
   Negative: waste; suffocating; tears; cry; broken; dark; dragged; discordant; lie; disappeared; uncomfortably; warning; caution; foolish; impulsive; bad; agitators; pain
3. I think the tone is **negative**. I see this in the passage when it says '**Mum always brought up the dress when issuing warning or caution about foolish and impulsive behaviour**'. This makes the tone **negative** because **the words 'warning', 'caution', 'foolish', 'impulsive' are negative words.**
   I think the tone is **positive**. I see this in the passage when it says **'always wore red lipstick and a bright yellow print-flower dress which she'd bought brand new'**. This makes the tone **positive** because **the words 'red', 'bright', 'yellow', 'flower' and 'new' bring up images of positive, happy things.**
4. The writer's attitude to the subject: Mixed feelings.

Identifying how the text is communicated, pages 27–28

Technique	Example(s)	Why it is effective	How does this develop our understanding of the writer's purpose?
simile	The grey-dust mountains in the distance surrounded the valley like a group of old *kaumātua*	Because the mountains are being described as old, backward, traditional, watchful, like men, or, they are being described to remind us of wise and kind grandfathers who are always looking out for us, protective of us.	She feels trapped here in this place she's 'escaped' to and feels like her family are still watching her every move, judging her, or, even though she might be feeling lonely and a bit lost, she can gain comfort from the idea that the mountains are solid and secure and safe.
repetition	Something free ... something good	Emphasis on the word 'something' before the positive words 'free' and 'good'. This word, however, is non-specific/vague.	Mai doesn't know what her future holds but she is hopeful that it will be positive. However, the repetition of the word 'something' reminds us that there is still doubt/she hasn't yet gained the surety she is seeking by leaving home.
colour imagery/ use of adjectives	red lipstick bright yellow print-flower dress	Outlines how Aunty Shirl stands out from everyone else with the bright, full-of-life colours she wears – reflecting on how full of life she is compared to everyone else.	In contrast to the grey of the mountains, which make Mai felt trapped, the memory of Aunty Shirl is positive and emphasises the idea that being different, radical, breaking away from the norms/restrictions of traditions is a positive thing.
personification	working of the wind gently stroking	The mountain/plants are alive.	She sees the land as being a part of her family/a part of her (her parents have a farm; she is Māori so holds the belief of the whenua being a person). That all of the land is there to take care of her like her family/mother did.
listing	Being here, being with the other women, meeting Tom, discovering herself	Makes more convincing by building up examples/by providing a number of reasons, adds weight.	She has been trying to justify whether her decision to leave home to come to work here is a good thing and this list is used to convince her all the reasons it was a good idea.
present continuous verb	**Being** here, **being** with the other women, **meeting** Tom, **discovering** herself	Gives the sense that the action is happening now/is ongoing/sense of anticipation or uncertainty.	We are right with Mai as she is learning about her new experiences.

ISBN: 9780170424547

Putting it all together, pages 28–29

Maiora has mixed feelings about her surroundings. The dominant tone of the first part of the extract is sad with words such 'waste', 'suffocating', 'tears', 'cry', 'broken', 'dark' because even though it appears she is having fun, she also thinks some negative things: being caught stealing tobacco, the hard work of the farm. One way the writer communicates this tone is to use a simile to describe what the mountains look like to Mai: 'The grey-dust mountains in the distance surrounded the valley like a group of old *kaumātua* ...' Because the mountains are being described as old, backward, traditional, watchful, like men, she feels trapped here in this place she's 'escaped' to and feels like her family are still watching her every move – judging her. **This idea is reinforced by the use of the rhetorical question when Mai remembers what her mother says of her Aunty Shirl: 'Do you want to end up like her?' A question she needs to consider for herself. Because it is her mother asking (expecting a no, she doesn't want to end up like Aunty Shirl), this alerts the reader to the idea that maybe Mai *will* want to end up like her aunt.**

In comparison to the 'grey-dust mountains' that surround the valley (and Mai), the writer uses more adjectives to describe Mai's Aunty Shirl: 'red lipstick, 'bright yellow print-flower dress'. This emphasises how Aunty Shirl stands out from everyone else with the bright, full-of-life colours she wears – reflecting on how full of life she is compared to everyone else. **In contrast to the grey of the mountains, which make Mai feel trapped, the memory of Aunty Shirl is positive and emphasises the idea that being different, radical, breaking away from the norms/restrictions of traditions is a positive thing.**

However, the writer also uses the listing of adjectives to describe the mountains in a positive way: 'silent, strong, reliable', which builds on the idea that she feels safe being able to see the mountains or that she feels safe because they remind her of her elders (kaumātua) **and so she likes the idea of them (her tūpuna) still being with her. She may be away from home but she is not 'away' from her ancestors.** Also, the writer using the simile to describe the valley – 'looked like the flat belly of an unevenly tanned sleeping man' – gives a dreamy quality and as if the valley is alive. The effect of this is to remind us the land is living and quietly lying there – **that we need to be careful not to 'disturb' the land, in the same way someone should take care not to disturb someone who is sleeping peacefully. This idea is developed by the use of the personification 'The continuous working of the wind stroking gently the plants in the valley below imitating breathing, a dreamer shuddering'. Mai sees the land below like Papatūānuku (Earth Mother) – nurturer, life-giver, which is why she describes what she sees in a positive way.**

This positive feeling is also communicated to the reader by the use of repetition: 'Something free ... something good', with the emphasis on the word 'something' before the positive words 'free' and 'good'. This word is non-specific because Mai doesn't know what her future holds but she is hopeful that it will be positive. However, the repetition of the word 'something' also warns the readers that there is still doubt and that perhaps Mai hasn't yet gained the surety she is seeking by leaving home.

The extract finishes with Mai reflecting on her aunt, not the tobacco farm down in the valley. By listing positive things ('Being here, being with the other women, meeting Tom, discovering herself') and using 'ing' verbs (being, meeting, discovering), there is a sense that Mai is breaking free from the confines of her traditional family and that this new life is happening now and is ongoing.

The writer is suggesting that for a young person, not sticking with tradition is healthier than being trapped doing meaningless work (like picking tobacco or working on the family farm), and that maybe children need to get away from their families to find out who they are. This story is set in 1962 during the time of much societal change: women's rights movement, black civil rights, and also a struggle in New Zealand for better conditions for Māori.

NARRATIVE PROSE 5: Aging Backwards

Pages 30–31

The writer reflects on the impact of her grandfather's aging by asking rhetorical questions such as, 'Why does he put Dad through this pain? Can't he see my dad flinch when he gets his name wrong?' which she provides the answers to using a short sentence: 'Sadly, no.' This abrupt answer to her questions pulls us up in our perhaps **(pointless)** hope that things will get better. **They won't. Aging means a continues journey towards death and usually is accompanied by illness and disappointment.**

The writer is both frustrated with her aging grandfather and sad that dementia and old age has taken so much, not only from him, but from her own father as well. **To her, the aging process is bad because it hurts close family members.** For example, we see specifically the hurt the writer sees when the grandfather forgets her dad when she says, 'my body strains as it ices over'. This metaphor emphasises that even though she wants to save her dad or even fix what's happened, she knows she can't, so does nothing and is frozen on the spot. **The writer believes that aging and all the negative effects are inevitable and perhaps we should not try to change things but learn to manage the altered life.**

As a way of describing the impact of her grandfather's aging, the writer uses similes such as 'Like tiny pin pricks, it pierces my heart'. We can see that the hurt is tiny but the fact that it is against the heart **(one of the most essential organs of a body)**, we can understand that although each time the grandfather forgets her father is usually something minor (like a look lacking in recognition), it still hurts a lot because it affects the emotional seat (the heart) of a person. **The reason for this is to communicate that sometimes families still suffer when their loved ones age even if they are not necessarily obviously ill (like with a stroke or cancer). Old age brings with it many small sorrows and, because even though everyone should accept that this is the way we will all probably go, it is still hard.**

Despite this, the writer also is quite positive about her grandfather. She describes him using positive, powerful adjectives, for example when she says, 'He is a big man, strong shoulders as broad as a picture frame.' Using the simile as well emphasises the 'larger than life' presence that grandfather has had in their lives. The words 'big', 'strong', 'board' further emphasise the fragility of his mind when she uses the metaphor to describe his 'grey eyes which are dusted with that layer of mist'. **We know that the eyes are the windows to the soul and if this has happened to her grandfather (his eyes are now covered), then not only can the family not see 'into' his mind, but he can't see out.**

ISBN: 9780170424547

The writer's attitude to the subject is also one of sadness and reminiscence. To her, the specific naming of the book (*Oliver Twist*) and the music (*English Country Garden*) creates a sense of the situation being bittersweet. Even though her grandfather has lost his short-term memory, the use of the specific proper nouns highlights that these older, traditional things are still remembered by her grandfather. The grandfather used to be a linguist and reader and a singer. **Not all has been lost and it is wonderful that the beauty of books and music can still bring happiness to her aging grandfather. This situation reminds us that there is still something we can do to bring light and joy to those who are old and/or suffer from memory loss. The writer suggests that we should not be so concerned about ourselves perhaps, but should put our own feelings to one side and focus on the older person.**

NARRATIVE PROSE 6: Recognition

Pages 32–33

The writer communicates her feelings about her family home through the use of parallel structure: 'The house looks bigger; the bricks brighter; the windows clearer.' This parallel structure and use of words with positive connotations makes the reader feel excited for the narrator; we know that there are changes and we look forward to seeing what they are. **Often, change is seen as a positive thing**. However, this parallel structure is then immediately contrasted with the negative words in the imagery in the following lines of 'trodden grass, cigarette butts and dumped concrete'. **The negative words allow us to learn that Ryan is not feeling happy about the changes to her family home. This is emphasised when she avoids going inside but instead walks around the house. Ryan is delaying the fact that 'things have to move on'. This is a common reaction to events that we don't want to face; sometimes change can be scary, as humans often fear the unknown. As a reader we can relate to how Ryan is feeling because we have all gone back to a place that once brought us happy memories only to see the changes that time has made: even places like our old primary schools, playgrounds, family holiday spots. Seeing change sometimes feels like the new view is taking something precious from the memories we have.**

We learn that Ryan feels very connected to her family home, which we see through the listing of major family events that have happened here: 'My dad grew up here; my uncle's ... My brother and uncle ... My grandmother ... my grandfather's ...'. **The repeated use of the personal pronoun 'my' and the listing of family members and events emphasise to us the closeness and ownership that Ryan feels towards this house. It reinforces the idea that she isn't happy about the changes that have happened and helps us understand her hesitation to walk inside the building.** We learn that this house is in Christchurch, as Ryan states that 'the Christchurch earthquakes have sped up the inevitable'. **This statement allows us to infer that Ryan has been through some form of trauma with the earthquakes and realise that Ryan knows that change is the only permanent thing about life, something in which we often have no choice.** She titles her piece 'Recognition' and the word is repeated throughout the piece. She seems to be in denial with the statement, 'I never thought that could happen.' But by the time we get to the end of the piece, Ryan has stopped referring to the building as a home but rather as a house. **She has made a conscious decision to disconnect her feelings and memories from the house and 'to move on'. Ryan's purpose in this piece is to share that it is normal to have a loss of control over aspects of your life and that it is okay to feel sad about it. But that we must face our sadness, recognise it, and then move on. It doesn't make the memories any less important just because the setting they occurred in has changed.**

POETRY

POETRY 1: The Trees

Pre-reading activities, pages 34–35

1 **a** Answers will vary.
b The: a definite article; talking about a specific thing.
Trees: plants with a single stem or trunk going to a considerable height – plural, so multiple plants; nature, large, strong, forest, green, lush, ...
2 Answers will vary.

Reading the poem, pages 35–36

2 Answers will vary.
3 Positive: buds; recent; relax; spread; greenness; born; again; new; thickness; fullgrown; May; afresh
Negative: grief; old; die; trick; new; unresting; thresh; thickness; dead
4 I think the tone of *The Trees* is **positive**. I see this in the poem when it says '**The trees are coming into leaf' and ends with 'Begin afresh, afresh, afresh.**' This makes the tone **positive** because **these are words that represent newness, life and fresh beginnings, all positive connotations.**

Linking the title with the end of the poem, page 36

1 The trees last year is dead they seem to say, begin afresh, afresh, afresh.
2 It tells us that there are always opportunities to start over and more on from the past.

ISBN: 9780170424547

Unpacking the text, page 37

1

Stanza	Summary
1	New leaves have sprouted on the trees, replacing the buds, which suggest that it is springtime.
2	Trees age each year like we do and the age rings are inside the trees.
3	Trees don't hold on to the things in the past but renew themselves each year.

a This poem is about how trees, like us, have a life cycle and that despite our time on earth being limited, we should carry on, like the trees, which 'refresh' themselves each year.

b The writer/speaker wanted to teach us about **how all living things 'wear' life's milestones** because **it happens to all of us – we have birthdays and get old and grey and, although trees 'hide' their rings inside, they too are aging. So, don't worry about getting old. Take comfort from the beauty of trees, which don't show concern for the ongoing cycle of life.**

Identifying the 'point of change', page 38

1 Line 4
2 Line 9
3 Positive, descriptive, fresh
4 Coming, almost, recent, buds, relax, greenness
5 Acknowledge the reality that although they appear brand new in May, the reality is that trees are also growing old and will die.
6 The tone of the poem is affirming and encouraging, that like the tree we can begin afresh as our life progresses.
7 Because the poet wants to mimic how life goes through cycles of change and sometimes we feel negative, and we are always getting older, but we can 'begin afresh'.

Identifying how the poem is communicated, pages 38–39

1 Simile: The trees are coming into leaf/like something almost being said
Metaphor: yet still the unresting castles thresh
Rhyme: leaf/grief, said/spread; again/grain, too/new; thresh/afresh (a-b-b-a)
Sibilance: afre**sh**, afre**sh**, afre**sh**
Personification: they seem to say
Verb: relax; spread; thresh
Assonance: unr**est**ing...thr**esh**
Personal pronoun: their; they
Repetition: afresh, afresh, afresh
Alliteration: **gr**eenness/**gr**ief; **l**eaf/**l**ike; **re**cent buds **re**lax; **s**eem to **s**ay
Question: Is it that they are born again/And we grow old?

2

Technique	Evidence	Effect	Purpose
question	Is that they are born again/And we grow old?	Makes us stop and think and wait for the answer.	We reflect on our questioning about growing old and look to compare our answers with the poet.
alliteration	**gr**eenness ... **gr**ief **l**eaf/**L**ike **r**ecent buds **r**elax **s**eem to **s**ay	Draws attention to both words to set up a contrast between them.	E.g. there is a juxtaposition of the image of greenness (new beginnings) and grief (the end of things) to remind us that life continues on and that there is always someone/something that has a fresh hope.
assonance	unr**est**ing ... thr**esh**	Emphasises the words and idea of movement.	Draws our attention to these two words so that we can be reminded of the harshness of what happens when we try to fight the natural order of things.
repetition	afresh, afresh, afresh	Shows how important the word is.	Draws our attention to this word which is the key idea that humans, like the trees, will be renewed or that we can have a chance to start again.
sibilance	afre**sh**, afre**sh**, afre**sh**	Makes a sound similar to the wind.	Mimics the sound to emphasise the image of the leaves in the trees.
rhyme scheme	a-b-b-a	Draws our attention to the connection of the words that rhyme. Also establishes a pattern.	To remind us that trees, like us, have a life cycle of beginnings and endings. That there is a circular nature of life.

ISBN: 9780170424547

Putting it all together, pages 39–41

The poet compares the life cycle of trees to the life cycle of people because he is saying that getting older is both a celebration of life but also an acknowledgement of inevitable death. When Larkin asks the question in the second stanza ('Is it that they are born again/And we grow old?'), he answers with a resounding 'No'. This short answer is his way of encouraging us not to be envious of the trees because they are still aging and in fact 'Their greeness is a kind of grief' – it is proof of another year passing, **just like how our celebrating a birthday is wonderful but also proof that we are getting older. The poet encourages us to be like the trees and not dwell on the past – that we can start 'afresh' – hence the reason he repeats this word and ends the poem with this word.**

By personifying the buds (which could be seen as a symbol for young people keen to grow up) – they 'relax and spread' – the poet is reminding us that living and dying is inevitable so we should not be in too much of a hurry or worry about this. Although trees appear to be born again by the renewing of the seasons, renewing of 'recent buds', the poet uses the metaphor 'yearly trick of looking new/Is written down in rings of grain' as a way of reminding us of the annual growth rings trees have. **He does this because he wants to say that trees are like us: we 'wear' life's milestones too. It's just that trees' rings are hidden inside them compared to ours being worn outside on our faces and bodies. Trees, unlike, people, can hide their age although nowadays, people often curate their social media presence to show only the 'greenness' of their lives.**

The soft sibliant sound in the repetition of the word 'afresh' makes us think of the 'swishing' sound of wind moving the leaves of trees. It is a familiar and comforting sound. **The reason for this is to end the poem with a recognition of our determination to keep going on because our time on earth is limited, to keep being renewed despite the death that awaits us all. This is further emphasised with the structure of the poem: the a-b-b-a rhyme scheme serves as an echo to the cyclical nature of life and death; grief and regrowth. The rhythm created by this rhyme scheme also serves to reflect the beat of a funeral march. The purpose of this is to ensure we don't forget that, despite the hope of being 'refreshed', we, like the trees, will still one day come to an end.**

The whole poem is an extended metaphor and also a piece of wisdom for living: Larkin uses his reflections of the trees as an examination of our own mortality and how, despite knowing this inevitability, we are determined to carry on despite – or even because of – this awareness that our time on earth is limited.

Just as the human race continues to renew through offspring, so do the trees. He communicates this idea right at the start of the poem by using the present particle verb 'coming' in the first line. The poet sets up the idea of continuous movement with this 'ing' word to emphasise the inevitability of growth, and a sense of ongoing life. This links to the last line of the poem where the repetition of the word 'afresh' emphasises this first idea of a never-ending life cycle.

POETRY 2: Anytime is Wrong Time and so is In-Between Time

Pre-reading activities, page 42

1 **a** Connotations will vary.

Word	Literal	Connotations
Anytime	Regardless of a date/time system	Flexible, fluid, willing to cater to another person's needs, reliable, easy-going
Wrong	Not in accordance with what is right or good	Negative, mistake, at fault, to blame
Time	System of measuring how long something is (duration)	Responsibility, date, clock, later, pressure, organised
In-Between	Being between one thing and another	Unsure, indecisive, transit, choices, unsure

b Someone who is really busy; someone who is inbetween jobs; inbetween job and social life

Reading the poem, pages 43–44

2 Answers will vary.
3 Negative: wrong; die; not;, cannot; unveiling; please; meeting
4 Positive: Christmas; New Year; Labour Day; Queen's Birthday; please; brother; whānau; gathering; right; right-time
5 Dominant tone is negative.

Linking the title with the end of the poem, page 44

1 Anytime is Wrong Time and so is In-Between Time; except right-time huis
2 Answers will vary. The poet is feeling sad and guilty (and a bit mad about feeling guilty) that he is expected to (but can't) go to family hui.

ISBN: 9780170424547

Unpacking the text, pages 44–45

1 The 'My opinion' section will have a variety of answers.

Stanza	Summary	My opinion	Which world?
1	During public holidays there is time for catching up.	I agree with this; it is great that everyone is on holiday around the same time.	Pākehā
2	Doesn't want grandmother to die when there is no time to spare (public holidays to ensure time off work)		Māori
3	Catches up with father on public holidays		Pākehā
4	Doesn't want pāpā to put pressure on him by asking him to come home.		Māori
5	Never a right time to meet with his brother		Pākehā
6	Doesn't want any funerals or gatherings at times that are not public holidays. He is happy for positive gatherings at times that suit him.		Māori

2 The poet feels **torn** about family gatherings because **if they don't fall on public holidays, he feels negative pressure to get the time off work and to get to his family.** We see this when the poet says '**I cannot come/anytime but these [which refers to 'At Christmas and New Year', which are public holidays**].'

3 Answers will vary. The key thing is a convincing response to 'Why?'.

Identifying the 'point of change', page 46

1 Line 21

2 Not including/but

3 Ihimaera is telling us that the right time to visit family is only when it's positive, such as birthdays and Christmas and/or when it's allowed by the public holidays.

4 Suggested answer: This shows us that holding a job far from family restricts the time you get to spend with them (or can be used as an excuse not to spend time with them).

Identifying how the poem is communicated, pages 46–47

1 Imperative: do not die
Lack of punctuation: At Christmas ... except right-time huis
Hyphenated word: between-time; wrong-time
Use of proper noun: Christmas; New Year; Queen's Birthday; Labour Day
Personal pronoun: me; I
Use of te reo Māori: taku kuia; taku pāpā; taku whānau
Structure: six stanzas: 1, 3 and 5 are three lines each and aligned to the margin; 2, 4 and 6 are four lines each and indented
Repetition: do not; anytime; wrong-time; brother; huis

2 Some suggestions:

Technique	Example(s)	Effect
proper noun	Christmas; New Year Queen's Birthday Labour Day	As New Zealanders, we know that these are public holidays where most businesses are shut. These are holidays that are attached to the Pākehā world.
personal pronoun	me; I	Makes us feel like the poet is speaking directly to us and begging us not to put any pressure on him to return home.
use of te reo Māori	taku kuia; taku pāpā; taku whānau	Allows us to know that this poem is set in New Zealand and that the poet is of Māori heritage. It contrasts with the use of proper nouns in the odd stanzas.
structure	six stanzas: 1, 3 and 5 are three lines each and aligned to the margin; 2, 4 and 6 are four lines each and indented	Emphasises the difference between work life and home life (heritage). The fact that the stanzas about his work life are on the margin and the Māori ones are 'pushed' across the page suggests that in order to keep a job, the poet must push aside his Māori heritage.
repetition	do not; anytime; wrong-time; brother; huis	Emphasises the point that the poet feels pressure to return home but there is no right time for him to do this.

Putting it all together, pages 47–49

The writer communicates his feelings about going home through the use of physical structure of how he has arranged the stanzas in this poem. The poet has deliberately alternated his stanzas between referencing the Pākehā and the Māori worlds. We can see this by both the language he uses and the physical displacement of every second stanza: in the first stanza the poet says 'At Christmas and New Year/there's time to spare' and in the next stanza he uses te reo when he says 'taku kuia do not die/between-time please'. We can see that in the first stanza the poet references public holidays of the Pākehā world whereas in the second stanza he talks about his Māori world and whānau.

ISBN: 9780170424547

This structure repeats throughout the poem, as every second stanza is displaced to the right to show the physical divide between the two ethnicities. **By arranging the poem in this way the poet is helping to communicate the conflict he feels between his work and living in the Pākehā world and his Māori life he had to leave behind. This shows us how he is apprehensive towards going home because he is confused about what he should prioritise — his work or his family. The fact that the stanzas about his work life are on the margin and the Māori ones are 'pushed' across the page suggests that in order to keep a job, the poet must push aside his Māori heritage. The effect on the reader is that we see how in his trying to fit into the New Zealand society that has its prejudices against Māori people and its traditions, he feels he has to sacrifice his people and heritage in order to make his mark on the world.**

Because the poet is feeling the pressure of being called home, he repeats the words which are like a refrain in his guilty conscience. Every time he gets the message to go home, it feels 'wrong' because whichever he chooses to do will disappoint someone. **If he stays at work, people like his brother will be on his mind, judging him perhaps; if he goes, he feels like those in the Pākehā world will judge him because of the hui he has to attend. By putting a Pākehā plural ('s') on the Māori word 'hui', the poet is telling us that his culture is so significantly affected by the dominating culture, the grammar of the language is made to follow the rules of the Pākehā world and not the Māori world.**

POETRY 3: Pussy Cat

Reading the poem, pages 50–51

2 and **3** Answers will vary.

Unpacking the text, page 51

1 Positive: visit; blue; orb; hands; poetic; Samoa; hips; lips; Her Majesty; centred; thorough; encompassing
Negative: frightened; big; drawl; blood red; inverting

2 I think the tone of 'Pussy Cat' is **positive**. I see this in the poem when it says '**Encompassing all the rest**'. This makes the tone **positive** because **the word 'encompass' means to gather together, circle around as if protecting and gives the impression of a big hug.**

Identifying how the poem is communicated, page 52

1

Technique	Evidence	Effect	Purpose
listing	moana blue Mena, ... Plantation House shawl ... paua orb ...	Overwhelms the reader of all the things the poet believes frightened the 'Western world'.	To emphasise how many things the poet believes the West thinks is scary about being Polynesian.
metaphor	I centred Polynesian navigation drawing a circle	Describes the way the poet rearranged the telling of the historical accounts to be at the centre of the world view. Describes how the message she is conveying is like the physical act of putting a ring around the world.	Underlines her message that London is not the 'centre' of the world but that the world is circular – no one person or people groups is more important than another.
question	Where have you been? What did you there?	Creates a tone of uncertainty or is a challenge for the 'listener' to justify what they have been up to.	People always want to know why we do what we do. These are simple questions but their answers are significant in that the place she went to (London) and what she did (visit the Queen) are massive and not things many people from the Pacific would expect to happen.
repetition	My Pussy cat	Draws attention to importance of these specific words. Mimics the traditional English nursery rhyme. Something we are familiar with.	This is her story; her account; her experience. The pussy cat repetition highlights the idea that a cat is seen as non-threatening (like the peoples who have been colonised) but like the poet, the cat picks on (frightens) a little mouse unexpectedly like the poet does with her Pacific 'claws'.
alliteration	**W**estern/**W**orld/**w**ith **s**iva/**S**amoa/hand**s**	Draws attention to these words by creating a sound connection to the images presented in the poem.	The sound of the alliteration is one of rhythm and is also an answer to the 'Where have you been' and 'What did you there' questions, so the alliteration connects the question with the answer – not just London but all of the West. The 'sibilant' sound of the 's' could be likened to the sound of the sea around the Pacific Islands and is soothing to a Pasifika person but maybe not so to those from the West who may think it is a dangerous sound like a snake.

ISBN: 9780170424547

Technique	Evidence	Effect	Purpose
allusion	Pussy cat, pussy cat/Where have you been?	Reminds us of the nursery rhyme.	It is a story we are familiar with, just like the idea of colonisation by England of the Pacific that we are familiar with. We know that the cat upsets things in London and that's was the poet says she has done as well.
rhyme	there ... hair shawl ... drawl lips ... hips West ... Best ... rest	Connects the words and draws attention to them and makes us consider what the similarities and differences are between the words.	The poet highlights the difference between the ideas presented in these words, which emphasises the difference between her world and the world of the West.

Putting it all together, pages 53-54

The poet firstly criticises the West when she *lists* all the Polynesian things that 'frightened the Western world' such as her 'big hair', 'moana blue Mena', 'Niu Ziland drawl', 'Va philosophising', etc., and *repeating* the word 'My' to show these things belong to her and her culture. All these things are actually positive aspects coming from the Pacific and we know are nothing to be frightened of – they are just clothing and dancing and thinking and speaking.

What she means is the West is frightened of things it does not know and by relating the words to the nursery rhyme of being frightened of a mouse – something that is not dangerous but of which people are still afraid – she is pointing out how silly they are to be frightened of something that cannot hurt you.

Another way she criticises the West is by using the *questions* from the nursery rhyme, 'Where have you been?' and 'What did you there?' This is effective because she did go to London and visit the Queen of England and she did 'frighten' the listening audience with her difference. So we can think it is kind of funny that they might be afraid of things which are familiar to us but not to people living in London. **The reader is challenged to think about the reasons we are really afraid of things. We, living in the Pacific, know that the things she lists are not frightening but rather a wonderful part of Polynesian culture. However, the audience is frightened just like those colonisers two hundred years ago who tried to stamp out the Pasifika culture because they didn't like difference, believing that 'West is Best' and everything else is inferior and therefore they believed they were justified in their terrible actions towards the native people. The poet was reminding her audience at the Commonwealth Day Observance that the behaviour of their ancestors was foolish.**

However, the poet also encourages the West to change the way it views the whole world and not just see England as the centre of the world when she says 'Inverting West is Best/Instead ... the rest'.The use of *rhyme* of West/Best/rest and *describing the action* of a 'drawing a circle' shows that it is possible for the whole of the world to be 'Best' and that the rest of the world 'Encompassing' them. This *verb* has positive connotations of supporting and caring. **What she means is it is possible to 'invert' the way the West sees the rest of the world but not be frightened by that thought – rather that it can see itself as part of a whole picture. The way for this to happen is to be exposed to things not of the Western culture, such as paua, siva dancing, Va philosophising.**

The use of the *proper nouns* when she *lists* the key people involved (Her Majesty/Duke of Edinburgh/Polynesian) is effective because it emphasises how equally important they are. **The reader is challenged to think that whether you are a royal like the Queen of England or a New Zealand poet with Polynesian heritage, you are just as important and your ideas are just as valuable as each other's. For too long, indigenous people and their language and culture have been considered lower in value than that of the white 'West' and this had led to much suffering and destruction of communities, many of whom have 'lost' their language and/or culture as a result of Westernisation. The purpose of this poem is to report back to us where she had gone and what she had done there and to communicate her happiness that she got a chance to speak for us and challenge the West with their notions that they are better than us, which we know is just silly – like being frightened by a mouse.**

POETRY 4: Makara Beach, Spring

Reading the poem, pages 55–56

2 Negative: sliding; no special grip; arches; stalks; shade; rescued; waiting; botulism

3 Positive: happiness; good; flowers; daisies; counts; yellow; smile; picnic; shade; agree; rescued; share; yes; silk; gather; centre

4 Overall tone is positive; almost surprised at how much she is enjoying the morning at the beach.

Linking the title with the end of the poem, page 56

1 Makara Beach, Spring; The morning's a ball/of silk unwound about us. You gather/it back with me at its centre.

2 It tells us that the poet is feeling happy in the morning at the beach. She feels like she is the centre of the world of who she is with. Husband? Friend? Child?

Identifying the 'point of change', page 56

1 Line 6

2 She stops trying to describe happiness and how it surrounds her and instead starts listing what she can see and what she is doing at the beach. This listing shows us the variety of flora, animal life and ethnicities that make up New Zealand. She is trying to show us that we should enjoy being outside and observing life, and that this is happiness.

ISBN: 9780170424547

Identifying how the poem is communicated, page 57

Some suggestions:

Technique	Example(s)	Effect
personal pronoun	me her I've you we	Helps us feel like we are at the beach with the poet, that we are experiencing these things alongside her. Because this is a poem set in New Zealand, we can easily imagine these scenes from our own memories and experiences.
simile	... skin of happiness ... Like an olive round an anchovy's body. ... like Maggie's neck ... ... white as foam ... ... dark as the sea's centre ...	By comparing what she is seeing with everyday objects, we are able to clearly imagine what the poet is seeing and build the scene in our minds.
repetition	yellow, there's yellow	This puts emphasis on the colour. Yellow often symbolises happiness, so she is drilling it into our minds that happiness is everywhere that she lists.
parallel structure	A heron ... A bunch ... A Vietnamese child ... A tide of gorse	Parallel structure gives each idea in the sentence the same importance. We all know that herons and gorse are typically found in New Zealand, so by adding a Vietnamese child into this list, the poet is pointing out how New Zealand is a multicultural society, and it is also a typical thing to see people of other ethnic roots when out and about.
metaphor	skin of happiness; A tide of gorse; The morning's a ball/ of silk	Because we understand that skin covers our entire body, this metaphor emphasises how 'covered over' she feels with happiness. Comparing the vision of the noxious, scrubby prickles to covering the hills as if they are moving like a strong sea that cannot be stopped.
personification	Blue eye daises	To make it feel as if they are looking at the poet/the scene as well creating the effect that the landscape is alive.

Putting it all together, pages 58–59

The writer uses the setting of Makara Beach, in spring, to communicate her view of New Zealand's society as a wonderful place to live and that we have a lot of variety to be enjoyed. Kidman starts her poem off with a series of similes such as 'Like an olive round an anchovy's body' through which she is trying to describe what happiness is and how it surrounds her in this moment. This immediately starts the poem off with a positive tone and we know that Kidman is happy to be where she is, on Makara Beach in spring. She then uses alliteration in the line 'But god, it's good, ...' to emphasise the point that she feels happy and that she thinks New Zealand is a great place to be. Kidman makes a point of repeating the word 'yellow' – 'and yellow, there's yellow/flora all over the place' – to emphasise how happy she is in this moment. **Yellow has connotations of a happy colour and so this repetition of the word links to her overall view of New Zealand society.** Kidman uses listing and parallel structure to help us see what she is seeing: the 'Blue eye daisies ... silver edged/leaf. A heron ... A bunch of overland cyclists ... Indians picnic ... A Vietnamese child ... A tide of gorse'. This is a snapshot of New Zealand, as all of the visual images that Kidman lists are typical New Zealand scenes, so as an audience we are able to relate to these immediately. **Kidman combines parallel structure with her listing to add equal importance to her observations.** Kidman deliberately lists the ethnicities of Indian and Vietnamese to show the readers that New Zealand is becoming an increasingly diverse society and that soon, as familiar as the gorse and the daisies are to us, seeing people of different ethnic origins will be also. **Because Kidman sandwiches these observations between mentioning happiness, we know that she feels positive about the things that she sees happening in New Zealand society.** **Even though daisies and gorse are technically weeds, to her they are beautiful and make the landscape even better by being there even though they are foreign. Just like some New Zealanders complain about certain ethnicities coming to New Zealand and spoiling things, she thinks the variety of cultures adds colour and life to our society. The irony is, many of those who complain about 'introduced' peoples are actually also descendants of immigrants.** She has also deliberately put the word 'Spring' in the title. Spring has connotations of new beginnings and freshness. Kidman seems to be saying that this current state of New Zealand society is only in its spring, its beginning. She believes that as New Zealand moves into its multicultural future, it will be a great place to be.

POETRY 5: Advice to a Discarded Lover

Pages 60–61

In relationships, we can be blinded by love and brush off rude comments from the partner or abuse because some of us can be manipulated by people (or even be the one who does the manipulation). **The poet shows this idea in her poem and her concern that people often make up with the other person, believing (wrongly) everything will be okay.** The way the writer presents her advice is not in a gentle way, which is what we might expect from someone 'giving advice', but is direct and harsh. One way she does this is with imperatives such as when she says 'Do not ask me for charity now' and 'Go away until your bones are clean.' The strength of the command in this advice suggests that the poet has the upper hand in the relationship. The imperatives are in the negative – 'Do not' and 'Go away' – but there is a hint of hope in the second one: she's giving the partner the option of coming back into her life, **suggesting that she acknowledges that people can change, but after seeing how harshly she described the relationship, it's showing she may be blinded by love.**

ISBN: 9780170424547

She is insulting him the whole poem, saying he reminds her of a dead bird, full of maggots. Saying that they have a dead affair, gruesome, and unpleasant. **By personification of the abstract nouns of 'self-pity' and 'pathos' ('You are eaten up by self-pity,/Crawling with unlovable pathos'), the poet makes the ideas active participants in what the problem is.** This imagery is disgusting and emphasises what she thinks is wrong with him, what he needs to fix about himself, by himself. Pathos is a quality that evokes pity and sadness. She's saying that he's full of this unlovable quality. I think that this is her way of telling him that she still cares but that she isn't going to stand and watch him behold this quality. **She wants him to be better, to be healthy, but she isn't going to be with him until he fixes what is wrong with him**. Even the 'Discarded Lover' in the title highlights this attitude. 'Discarded' means something you don't want any more, but a 'lover' is a person that you love and care about. These two words are almost opposites but she uses them together. **This makes me think that maybe she just doesn't want him right now, but might do again one day.**

This poem encourages the ex-lover (and the reader) to make sure that the hurt and messy feelings are truly dead so that they can properly communicate with each other. She does this through the extended metaphor of the decaying bird when she says 'Returning later, though, you will see/A shape of clean bone, a few feathers,/An inoffensive symbol of what/Once lived. Nothing to make you shudder' and 'If I were to touch you I should feel/Against my fingers fat, moist worm-skin.' **The second quote, especially the adjectives of 'fat' and 'moist', shows the anger and frustration she holds against her partner because of the break-up, but then she says 'Go away until your bones are clean', relating to the first quote: the 'inoffensive' remains of the dead bird after the decay and rotting is over. This means that they should come back into contact with one another when all those feelings are gone and they can properly communicate.** This would be so useful for broken-up couples and would reduce the amount of emotional strain on them. I hear stories about how couples have broken up, but they're still fighting, and I wonder: why are they fighting if the relationship is over? I think it would be impossible not to fight because you obviously had to break up over something, and that something will always be the subject of frustration for you both until those feelings die. **The poem advertises the importance of staying away in order to let those feelings die, otherwise we'll all be in emotional despair for a long time over that relationship that didn't work out. After reading this poem, I realised that you will never lose that deep bond or connection after you end a relationship; it's only the feelings that go away. This would be a good lesson to learn for those couples who think that there is no hope that the situation will get better. Degradation of the relationship is the natural severing of emotional ties with the other person. For people to recognise this will help them find their bearings/where they stand in the process of the severing and comfort them because someone else in this world relates and has been through it. They can be assured that all those feelings are normal and, as a result, they can better control them.**

POETRY 6: And if it snowed

Pages 62–63

The writer uses a rhyme scheme of a-b-a-b and parallel structure to show that people's characters can be complex and that domestic violence can occur anywhere. The poem starts off by showing the subject in a positive manner, that when it snows 'he took a spade and tossed it to one side'. This imagery causes us to think of the character as a strong man, who is willing to do physical labour and work in the cold to help people. Three of the four lines start with the word 'And'. This parallel structure creates a sense of listing, which shows us the different aspects of the subject's character. The word 'lied' then rhymes with the word 'side'. **Because of this rhyme, the lines fit together and we aren't shocked at the fact the subject 'slippered' his daughter. As well as the rhyme scheme, the choice of the word 'slipper' has positive connotations, as slippers are a comfy, soft shoe. We imagine that she got a soft smack on the bottom and that she probably deserved it for lying.**

In the second stanza, the parallel structure and positive imagery continue to build up an image in our minds of the subject being a good man. He saves some of his pay cheque and he praises his wife for her cooking. This then makes the break from the rhyme scheme at the end of the stanza, all the more shocking to us. We are expecting to read another positive line about this man but instead we read 'And once, for laughing, punched her in the face.' **The shock that this line and the break from the rhyme scheme has on us is deliberate, as it mimics the shock that happens to the victim of domestic violence and often the shock to those who find out it has happened. Usually, perpetrators of domestic violence are seen as positive members of the wider community and the public, and the victim is often not believed.** This is shown in the final stanza when Armitage states that 'they rated him ... sometimes he did this, sometimes he did that', not that he was an abusive husband and father.

The third and fourth/final stanza go back to the parallel structure and rhyme scheme and we find out that the subject looked after his ailing mother and hired her a nurse, but then, twice, he robbed from her purse. The fact that it is a small amount, 'ten quid', makes it all the more worse that he couldn't have just asked her for the money. **However, the fact that the worst abuse, of hitting his wife, is cocooned in the centre of the poem, between petty thieving and a (probable) light smack is deliberate. It means that as readers we find it hard to believe that the subject hit his wife. This effect on us is a mimic of what happens in society. Often, when a victim comes forward, people don't believe their claims, because of what they know to be good about that person. What Armitage is doing is proving to us that people are complex and have many layers. It might be that the person we least expect to be cruel and violent is the one doing it. Armitage wants us to consider what we know about the people around us and to make us consider that even if people sometimes do good things, they can also do bad things and that we should support and believe the victims. There is also a suggestion that he is challenging or criticising the reader/society for not doing more to stop this terrible abuse.**

NON-FICTION

NON-FICTION 1: We don't need our community to be grateful, we need them to be okay

Pre-reading activities, pages 64–65

1 **a** furore: an outbreak of public anger or excitement
b rehash: to reuse (old ideas or materials) without changing them
c charity: the voluntary giving of help, typically in the form of money to those in need
d paradigm: a typical example or pattern of something
e agency: a business, person or organisation providing service on behalf of another
f by-products: things that are produced during the production or destruction of something else
g prohibitive: (of a law or situation) forbidding or restricting
h demeaning: causing someone to lose their dignity/mana/respect
i dispense: to distribute or provide something or service to a number of people
j ostensibly: apparently; as appears or is stated to be true, though not necessarily so
k communist: a person who supports or believes in the principles of communism (i.e. equal distribution of wealth to all peoples in a society)
l disempowering: making a person or group (feel) less powerful or confident
m parental: (to be or to act) like a parent

2 I think the piece will be about **the government and their effect on people** because **of the selection of words: communist, parental, agency, furore, etc., which are all words mentioned in the news when bringing news about the people and a government.**
Our answers:

3 **a** To me, 'community' means a group of people coming together and supporting and accepting one another to help each other out.
b To me, 'to be okay' means not 100% but able to live comfortably without pressing worries.
c What ideas: governments/communities being kinder to their people because the word 'grateful' would imply that they should be grateful for what they've got, which is a hostile attitude from the government, whereas the phrase 'we need them to be okay' implies there should be support from those places.
d Answers will vary.

4 **a** If the people are getting enough support/enough of what they need and whether they are okay in terms of health, emotions, physical safety. I would think that others are their main concern, not their own needs.
b I think this piece will be about **helping people less fortunate than yourself** because **the writer is a spokesperson, speaking on behalf of the Aunties and the Women's Refuge, therefore (as they are charities) asking us to help them.**

Reading the text, pages 66–67

2 and **3** Answers will vary.

Unpacking the text, pages 68–69

1

1	The writer acknowledges she has created some controversy with her comments about charity.
2	We should trust that people know what they need to 'be okay', so let them choose the resources.
3	The way in which we speak can make a big difference as to how people in need feel about themselves.
4	Shows us the contrast between 'living in poverty' and 'deliberately under-resourced' and examines language differences.
5	The writer lists off what things contribute to people being in need.
6	The writer explains what the Aunties do and how they carry out their duties.
7	We need to move away from the old way of thinking about how to help people because that way makes people in need feel powerless.
8	We need to start giving selflessly and not expect anything in return: gifting.
9	The writer tells us to treat people in need as equals and not act like a parental figure.
10	In a community, everyone needs to 'be okay'.

2 **a** Even though the idea of charity is associated with being a good thing, giving in the wrong way can make the people we're giving to feel disempowered. We should be putting some choice back into the charity process. We can do this by letting them choose what they need instead of giving them random stuff (and we also need to stop thinking they should be grateful for whatever they get).
b The writer wanted to teach us **that there are lots of judgemental attitudes toward those in poverty and the people affected by it** because **we may not understand what those who work in and with charities deal with every day. They get distressed clients and have one-on-one contact, whereas we sit and give them money online. They've met who they're helping and hear them.**

ISBN: 9780170424547

Identify the 'call to action', pages 69–70

1–5 Answers will vary.

6 One answer is: According to this text, **you cannot understand a person until you have walked in their shoes**. We see this in the text when the writer says '**I decide who can use it because I have a relationship with them, or their social worker, and in the cases where I know the person directly, I ask them**'. This means **that she believes once you get to know them, you'll understand what they need and know that they will be grateful when offered it**. So, the writer wants us to **not judge but rather take the time to get to know someone who is in a different situation to you** so that we can **make people feel welcomed, supported and part of the community despite the struggles they are going through**.

Identifying how the idea is communicated, pages 70–72

Some suggestions:

Technique	Example(s)	Why it is effective	How does this develop our understanding of the writer's purpose?
personal pronoun	**I** started a bit of furore. **You** may have seen **it** ...	She's writing about her experience but, because she wants to engage in a conversation, she includes the reader as well.	So that we feel this issue of how we treat people who need our help becomes personal to us.
repetition	make their own choices/ making their own decisions	Drumming it into our heads that the agency is in the hands of those in need, but saying it more than once.	Emphasising the idea that they are the ones in control – not us.
imperative	Let's start with the language. Gift with love. Empower people ...	We cannot be passive in our response because she is commanding us to act. Also, starting with verb enhances the sense of urgency.	The writer is directing the line of discussion; we *have* to do what she says, which makes her have the upper hand and the reader more likely to follow the instructions.
colloquial language	telly stuff okay awful	The everyday conversational language mimics how friends might talk to one another, so this makes the reader feel that they are chatting with someone they can relax with/relate to.	Because nobody thinks of themselves as unkind, using this informal language makes it feel like we are on 'the same wavelength' as the writer and therefore we would be more responsive to the suggestions for changing the way we think and act.
jargon	charity; rent; agency; paradigm; economy; benefit; costs; resourced	All words directly associated with the topic of people who are struggling in our community.	These are likely to be used by politicians or those who perhaps might try to avoid discussing directly the reality of life in poverty, especially as one of the key ideas is the need to change the language that is used when talking about those in need.
listing	low wage economy, prohibitive rents, benefits that are set to be deliberately unlivable, and prohibitively high food costs mentioned on telly, on the radio, in the papers, or on social media	Makes more convincing by building up examples/by providing a number of reasons, adds weight. The list provides proof/evidence with multiple examples of problems (places the discussion was being held) to strengthen the writer's credibility to be able to discuss the problem with charity.	There are many reasons why people struggle, so the writer is trying to provide all the possible situations so that we can see just how big the issue is.
short sentence	All of us. To be okay. We can do that.	Adds to a short, sharp tone. Only the key ideas are said, which makes sure these ideas/words/phrases are separated so we can focus on the key message.	There is no need for long, drawn-out discussions or explanations for what the problem is or how to fix it. The solutions are easily seen (even if not easy to execute).

ISBN: 9780170424547

Putting it all together, pages 72–73

The writer explains why society must change the way it helps those in need through the use of an imperative. The writer uses an imperative when she says 'Let's start with language', 'Gift with love', 'Empower people'. We cannot be passive in our response because she is commanding us to act. **Also, starting with a verb enhances the sense of urgency. The writer is directing the line of discussion; we have to do what she says, which makes her have the upper hand and the reader more likely to follow the instructions. The writer is used to having to 'do battle' with people to get the help she needs for the people she works with and this comes across in the tone of the article – very directive and strong – which is what you need to be if you want to change a whole society's negative attitude to a disadvantaged group that has no power. It's hard changing people's deep-seated prejudices.**

Society has conjured up this image that when we give someone something, we expect a thank you or something nice in return and it's rude if you don't. The writer is commanding us to change our thinking, first by the language we use, which also comes from a change in attitude. **When you're giving someone something out of the goodness of your own heart, you really don't want anything in return because you know you've just done a good deed in your life. It also makes some people think they need to do something extravagant to say thank you, to go out of their own way even if they're in a place of struggling to do it and it's like 'No, you don't have to do that. Just appreciate it and we'll be satisfied – it's not about me [the gifter] but about you'.**

The writer also explains why society must change the way it helps those in need in order to encourage us as readers to initiate that societal change. The writer does this through the use of a rhetorical question: 'Because we're not in 1960s communist Russia, right?' This phrase highlights the similarities between what the writer has discovered between the function of oppressive governments such as the Soviet Union and the public's perception of how charities run. **Communist governments restrict the freedom of their citizens by limiting the choices they can make in life, including by distributing allocated portions of food and necessities to its people; much like how we see charities as groups simply handing out resources to people in need. By questioning us, the writer is forcing us to consider our own preconceived ideas about charities while at the same time suggesting that in some sense, charities have become like 1960s communist Russia. As this period was so notoriously brutal and controlling, this suggestion shocks us because charities are meant to help people.** The writer did this to show how charities have become simply about the donations and the 'stuff' the people are receiving. Through the use of a rhetorical question, the writer suggests that allowing vulnerable people freedom to make their own decisions is the most important thing.

She also uses a rhetorical question when she asks, 'When you go to the supermarket you take what you need, don't you?' By saying this she is making the point that the people in need should be able to choose what they need like at the supermarket to encourage them to get help when they need it rather than letting pride get in the way. **By giving those in need the chance to decide for themselves what they need, this gives them the opportunity to make important decisions in their life, which they don't have a lot of opportunity for, as 'beggars can't be choosers'. Right? Except that statement is demeaning and belittling. The writer's idea of letting those in need decide what they want/need (like a supermarket), helps them to regain control and their life, and the simple decision in deciding what they need can go a long way in helping them regain self-esteem, and prepare them for bigger, harder decisions they may have to make. Also by using a supermarket analogy, she is helping the readers to gain a better understanding as to why society must change the way help is given. By using an everyday (and necessary) place that the reader is familiar with, the reader is put into the shoes of those in need and is challenged to think about how we would feel in that situation and helps us to realise that society must change the way it helps those in need.**

Another way the writer explains why society must change the way it helps those in need is by the use of repetition. The writer asks 'how do we change the paradigm?' and later in the text says 'We can also shift the paradigm …', which is effective because repetition's role as a technique is to get something stuck in your head. We repeat something because that idea is so important you need to be reminded twice or more times about it. In this case, a paradigm means a typical example or pattern; basically it's another word for a stereotype because it's a typical example. She's meaning that society is stereotyping those in need and has the attitude towards the poor as 'they got themselves in that situation, then they can get themselves out'. **This attitude is negative and the repetition of the phrase highlights part of the problem – society sees the poor as disgusting people in society and shouldn't exist because they're not doing any good for the world.**

NON-FICTION 2: Assured, authentic Jacinda Ardern impresses overseas

Pre-reading activities, pages 74–75

1–3 Answers will vary.

Reading the text, pages 76–77

2 Answers will vary.

3 Hawkesby wants us, as New Zealanders, to **be kinder to our PM. Although she mocks her shoe choice, overall she is impressed with how she has conducted herself overseas and seems concerned that the New Zealand media is going to give her a hard time again once her baby arrives.**

ISBN: 9780170424547

Unpacking the text, pages 77–78

1

1	We have to give our PM a high score for her trip.
2	The author gives her top marks.
3	She didn't embarrass us with her clothes.
4	She wore the Māori cloak in a respectful way.
5	She conducted herself well.
6	She did better than the more experienced Camilla.
7	She did a great job, especially considering she is pregnant.
8	She was at ease with the royals.
9	It's amazing she was at ease, as she doesn't believe in the monarchy.
10	The British and European press said good things.
11	She didn't embarrass us.
12	She did great things.
13	Ardern can enjoy this positive press for a while, and, when her baby arrives, it will start up again.

2 **a** This piece is about Jacinda Ardern, our PM, and her trip to Europe. It begrudgingly praises her for the way she behaved and dressed, and seems surprised to find that Ardern didn't embarrass us.

b The writer wanted to teach us about **Ardern's success at CHOGM** because **we should appreciate that she did well and represented our country well, even if we don't agree that she should be our Prime Minister.**

Identify the 'call to action', pages 78–79

A: The universal truths according to the text	B: Our 'call to action'
A person who is genuine can be trusted.	Always be true to ourselves.
Sometimes the polite thing to do is pretend to be interested even when you're not.	Respect other people when they are speaking/sharing, even if it is boring to you.
You should always respect other people.	To treat others with respect.
We feel proud when someone from New Zealand does well on the international stage.	Strive to represent our country well when you can.
Do not always believe what the media has to say.	Be critical of information you can't verify.
People are judgemental.	Try not to care what people say about you.

2–5 Answers will vary.

6 One answer is: According to this text, **we should be respectful**. We see this in the text when the writer says, '**she managed to pull that [the kahu huruhuru cloak] off in a way that seemed respectful and natural**'. This means **that since Ardern showed respect to our Māori culture, she portrayed New Zealand in a good light**. So, the writer wants us to **be considerate and show respect to others regardless of race or gender** so that we can **have a more equal New Zealand society**.

Identifying how the idea is communicated, pages 80–81

1 Personal pronoun: I/we're
Imperative/command: Mark my words
Listing: female, young, pregnant, smiley, upbeat, positive
Proper noun: Camilla; Commonwealth Games
Use of te reo Māori: kahu huruhuru
Repetition: Chogm; shoes; Commonwealth; press
Short sentence: Mark my words.
Colloquial language: Kiwi designers; huge raps
Jargon: CHOGM; Allbirds; coup

ISBN: 9780170424547

2

Technique	Example(s)	Why it is effective	How does this develop our understanding of the writer's purpose?
personal pronoun	**I** think if **we**'re going to give the PM a score ...	She's writing about her opinion but, because she wants to engage in a conversation, she includes the reader as well.	So that we feel that this idea of rating our Prime Minister is something that we are all a part of.
imperative/ command	Mark my words.	It creates an order and makes the reader feel like they have no choice but to do as she says.	It grabs the reader with its intensity, preceding something important.
listing	female, young, pregnant, smiley, upbeat, positive	Creates dramatic effect because many points are being mentioned in quick succession. Emphasises Jacinda's qualities.	The writer is trying to get the reader to recognise Ardern's qualities and listing them makes the name of qualities greater. Also, mentioning many points in quick succession creates a dramatic effect to keep the reader interested.
proper noun	She pulled off what **Camilla** couldn't at the **Commonwealth Games** opening.	Proper nouns indicate a particular person or place and communicate an identifier. Helps build a specific image in the reader's mind.	Proper nouns are used here to compare Ardern to other well-known figures and to force us to draw a comparison between them, favourable to Ardern.
jargon	CHOGM; Allbirds; coup	Adds weight to Hawkesby's article as it makes us feel like she must know her stuff to use the jargon.	It makes us feel that Hawkesby is informed and educated and that we should listen to her opinion.
colloquial language	Kiwi designers; huge raps	Makes the article feel less formal and more like a friendly conversation so we can feel more in touch with Hawkesby.	It makes us feel that Hawkesby is a friend and that we should listen to and value her opinion.

Putting it all together, pages 81–83

The writer's attitude towards Jacinda Ardern is positive overall. Hawkesby admires her and how she represented New Zealand at CHOGM. This is shown in the text through the use of listing: 'female, young, pregnant, smiley, upbeat, positive, culturally aware and considerate'. **By listing these positive words to describe Ardern, Hawkesby makes the number of qualities seem large and this emphasises how much she admires her in this moment and pushes that we should admire her too.** **When you are focusing on a thing or a person, it's very easy to critically evaluate them. It's a bit disturbing that the list of adjectives the writer uses have as much to do with Jacinda's gender (not relevant) as her role as Prime Minister of New Zealand (relevant). This just emphasises how much harder a judge the world is for women in power because it is unlikely Bill English would have also been described as 'male, older, father of many, smiley' etc.** Hawkesby uses an imperative, 'we'd have to score her very highly', to drive home her point that Ardern deserves New Zealand to admire how she represented us on the world stage, even if you don't think she should be Prime Minister.

Hakwesby also expresses her positive attitude towards Ardern through the use of adjectives: 'Ardern's authenticity has served her well. She's looked at ease, conversational and chatty'. These positive adjectives help us to understand how Jacinda represented New Zealand in a positive and admirable way. This shows the reader that Hawkesby believes that Ardern's ability to be genuine made her trustworthy to the other world leaders. This teaches the reader that you should always be true to yourself, because when you are tyring or pretending to be something you're not, you won't come across as genuine, which is not beneficial.

NON-FICTION 3: Procrastination

Unpacking the text, page 85

1

1	I struggle with procrastination.
2	Procrastination is putting off doing something by engaging in time-wasting activities like watching a lot of television.
3	Social media is addictive and it's more interesting than doing homework.
4	The refresh button used on social media has been designed like a slot machine – to mimic the feeling one gets when gambling.
5	It's hard to give up social media but here are some suggested things you can do to cut down on your time using it.
6	You are a complex and valued organism and your time is worth protecting.

2 The speaker identifies that we all struggle with procrastination and that there is a risk we may be addicted to social media in the same way a gambler is addicted. She encourages us (with some practical examples) of things we can do avoid procrastination, which is often connected with our phone.

ISBN: 9780170424547

Identifying the 'call to action', page 86

A: The universal truths according to the text	B: Our 'call to action'
People will do almost anything to avoid painful or difficult work.	Recognise that it is normal to want to avoid hard tasks (procrastinate).
With a plan in place, you can achieve change.	Make a plan and stick to it.
Lots in this world distract us from doing meaningful things.	Understand what is happening around you and how we are being manipulated by social media companies.

2 According to this text, **lots in this world distract us from doing meaningful things**. We see this in the text when the writer says, '**social media companies are trying to get you as addicted to their app as some people are to gambling**'. This means **the designers of the social media companies use the refresh button in the same way gamblers use their devices – it is designed to keep us focused on their platform in the same way gambling apps are designed to keep people spending time and money**. So, the writer wants us to **be warned and understand what is happening around you and how we are being manipulated by social media companies** so that we can **take steps to avoid wasting precious time (and our lives) doing meaningless things like watching too many cat videos rather than important things like our education and spending time with our families**.

Identifying how the idea is communicated, page 87

Technique	Example(s)	Why it is effective	How does this develop our understanding of the writer's purpose?
personification	to kick this essay's butt	Helps us to imagine that the essay is something actively 'fighting' the speaker.	She wants to emphasise how hard she finds making herself sit down and write her essay, so by creating an image of the essay being something she is at war with, it helps us to understand the great effort she feels she needs to summon to finish her homework. Also, the phrase 'kick butt' is used to indicate that overcoming or winning *can* be achieved with the right attitude. You kick someone's butt when you are pushing them away from you and sending them on their way.
repetition	not good ... Not good ... not at all good	Highlights and emphasises that the impacts of social media are bad.	Three times the speaker says this, which reinforces her point that the way social media impacts our lives is bad.
imperative	Hide that phone! Close that tab! Just do it!	It's directed at the audience. Makes us part of the speech because she is giving us something to do.	Because the speech is encouraging us to stop procrastinating, these commands are part of the solution to do that. Procrastination, according to the speaker, is about avoiding action. These imperatives command us to act, not just be passive listeners.
personal pronoun	you we I us our your	Connects us to the speaker because she is speaking about herself and speaking to us, the listener.	The speaker is trying to persuade us and encourage us to avoid procastination and she does this by using her own personal experiences to illustrate what she is saying. She then directs her comments to the audience because her hope is that her words will help us with our own struggles with procrastination.
colloquial language/ cliché	zilch, zip, nada! butt that ball rolling	Conversational language is friendlier and therefore makes us feel like we are listening to someone we know.	It's easier to encourage a friend to change their behaviour than it is a stranger, so the speaker is addressing the audience as if she is giving advice to a friend – we are more likely to listen to someone we trust and be more willing to acknowledge our failings with procrastination to a friend than a stranger.
short sentence	Hide that phone! Close that tab! Just do it! Get this!	Sounds like somone snapping their fingers to get our attention.	Procrastination often causes us to get distracted by unnecessary things such as watching television or YouTube videos. We need to 'snap out of' our distractions and these short sentences are as if the speaker is standing in front of us while we are distracted and calling us to attention.
rhetorical question	but isn't that crazy?	We know the answer is yes but the question makes us think of it ourselves. When the answer is obviously the same as the speaker's, we feel validated and therefore more inclined to listen further.	The details she is drawing our attention to have no relevance to her topic and that is the point: doing something that has no purpose is 'crazy', just like procrastinating is crazy – a bad thing to do as it achieves nothing. Learning irrelevant facts when you're supposed to be doing an important task is not very wise.

ISBN: 9780170424547

Putting it all together, pages 88–90

The serious message the speaker wanted to get across to the audience is how bad procrastinating can be in terms of getting positive things done in your life. She understands that social media, in particular, is very time consuming and cites authorities who talk about the addictive nature of the 'refresh button' being like a gambling machine. **However, she uses a range of techniques designed to involve the audience and make them feel that she is understanding and on their side, rather than using a negative preaching manner/tone.**

According to this text, lots in this world distract us from doing meaningful things. We see this in the text when the speaker says 'social media companies are trying to get you as addicted to their app as some people are to gambling'. This means that the designers of social media companies use the refresh button in the same way gamblers use their devices – it is designed to keep us focused on their platform in the same way gambling apps are designed to keep people spending time and money. **So, the speaker wants us to be warned and understand what is happening around us and how we are being manipulated by social media companies so that we can take steps to avoid wasting precious time (and our lives) doing meaningless things like watching too many cat videos rather than important things like our education and spending time with our families.**

Procrastination often causes us to get distracted by unnecessary things such as watching television or YouTube videos. She uses short sentences and imperatives such as 'Hide that phone! Close that tab! Just do it!' and 'Get this!', which sounds like someone snapping their fingers to get our attention. **We need to 'snap out of' our distractions and these short sentences are as if the speaker is standing in front of us while we are distracted and calling us to attention. Also, because the speech is encouraging us to stop procrastinating, these commands are part of the solution to do that. Procrastination, according to the speaker, is about avoiding action, especially doing things which are hard, boring or which we don't like. These imperatives command us to act, not just be passive listeners.**

The speaker wants to emphasise how hard she finds making herself sit down and write her essay, so personifies the essay as something that has a 'butt' needing 'kicking'. By creating an image of the essay being something she is at war with, it helps us to understand the great effort she feels she needs to summon to finish her homework. **Also, the phrase 'kick butt' is used to indicate that overcoming or winning can be achieved with the right attitude. You kick someone's butt when you are pushing them away from you and sending them on their way. This personification 'to kick this essay's butt' helps us to imagine that the essay is something actively 'fighting' the speaker.** Also, it's easier to encourage a friend to change their behaviour than it is a stranger, so the speaker is addressing the audience using informal, colloquial language as if she is giving advice to a friend **because we are more likely to listen to someone we trust and be more willing to acknowledge our failings to a friend than a stranger.** This conversational language ('Oh yeah', 'Well, there you go') is friendlier and therefore makes us feel like we are listening to someone we know. **In the end, people will do almost anything to avoid painful or difficult work, so the speaker uses a variety of effective language features to help us to recognise that it is normal to want to avoid hard tasks (procrastinate) but, if we make a plan and start small, we will be able to overcome our procrastination.**

NON-FICTION 4: an abridged speech delivered by Maggie Rainey-Smith

Unpacking the text, page 92

1

1	It is an honour to speak at today's Anzac service as I do it on behalf of my father who was a World War II war veteran.
2	My father was from Kaikōura and happily went off to fight in World War II.
3	I have been to Maleme and seen the graves of the soldiers who died – mostly young Germans.
4	I visited Poland and saw where POWs like my father were kept.
5	The prisoners of war had to march 600 miles and many died.
6	My father suffered from PTSD (post-traumatic stress disorder) when he returned and I dreaded Anzac Days.
7	I can't separate war from my father and Anzac Day makes me feel connected to my family.
8	We have to remember the wives and families who are still suffering during current wars.
9	Anzac Day is not a time to think about whether it was the right thing to do, but to remember those who are left to remember.

2 The writer explains her connection to the Anzac Day remembrance service by talking about her father and acknowledging that the day is not just about the soldiers but their families as well.

Identifying the 'call to action', page 93

1

A: The universal truths according to the text	B: Our 'call to action'
Everyone suffers because of war.	We must do all that we can to help not only the returning soldiers but their families as well.
Time can change our attitude to things.	Be prepared to shift your perspective as you grow older.
Commemorations help communities connect.	Attend your local Anzac Day service.
People have different experiences of war.	Don't be quick to judge/criticise those who think differently to you.
War damages minds as well as bodies.	Be respectful of those who suffer depression and mental illness.

ISBN: 9780170424547

2 Our answer:

According to this text, **war damages minds as well as bodies**. We see this in the text when the writer says '**When my dad returned from the war he was diagnosed as having shell-shock, something that wasn't truly understood back then**'.This means **that his thinking and emotions were negatively affected by what he had experienced and, although the doctors had a name for it, it did not go far enough to show undertanding that this meant soldiers suffered terrible anxiety and depression**. So, the writer wants us to **be mindful that though a soldier may be a hero for the things they did in the war, and wear the medals as outward symbols of that action, we still need to understand that some wounds cannot be seen; we need to be respectful of those who suffer depression and mental illness** so that we can **help not only the returning soldiers but their families as well.**

Identifying how the idea is communicated, page 94

Technique	Example(s)	Why it is effective	How does this develop our understanding of the writer's purpose?
personal pronoun	Today **I** am here with **my** granddaughter ...	Makes it clear it is a personal account, which makes it more authentic because the writer is speaking from her experiences.	In recounting her experiences and explaining why she is here with her granddaughter, she is emphasising the ongoing effects of a soldier's choice to go to war – in this case her own father. It makes us think of our own family relationships, especially with those who have been affected by war.
pun	who is right/who is left	The play on words makes us appreciate the idea that there is often more than one response to a word or idea.	This is a play on the words 'right left' – the marching call for soldiers – and also the word 'right' meaning correct and the word 'left' meaning remnant, left over. The narratives around war and fighting are often to do with who won (or should have won), i.e. who was in 'the right', whereas the speaker is asking us to also remember those who were 'left behind' when the soldiers went to war and those who are 'left' now (descendants) of those who went to war. The effect of this is to reinforce that war has long-reaching consequences.
alliteration	connected to my community Germans who were also suffering and starving	We hear the similar sounds in the words making them link together.	Emphasises the ideas of communities being connected by a shared experience: Anzac Day The hissing sound in the phrase mimics perhaps how someone in pain might feel. By making it the Germans (who were the enemy at that time), we can sympathise with them that they too suffered, not just our soldiers.
quotation	'War does not determine who is right – only who is left.'	By including the words of a well-known, well-respected person, this adds weight/a sense of authority to the argument.	She and her granddaughter are part of those 'left'. She uses Bertrand Russell's famous quote to emphasise that she and others like her all around the world are the living example of what he says.
adjective	sheer young breathtaking haunting	Provides a more specific image of the thing the speaker is talking about. They are strong adjectives.	She is wanting us to picture in our minds what she saw when she visited Poland and Maleme, so that we can attempt to appreciate the devastation that war brings.
listing	my dad, the whiff of boot polish, the drumbeats that stir me so, the haunting Last Post, the sausage rolls after at the RSA Iraq, Syria, Yemen, Gaza and the Ukraine	Building up a picture of all the things she remembers.	By listing examples of things she remembers, the speaker reinforces the idea that, despite it being a long time ago now, such was the impact of war on her father (and her family), she still has very clear and specific memories of that time. This also enforces the idea that the 'end of the war' does not mean the end of its effects.

ISBN: 9780170424547

Putting it all together, page 95

The speaker provides a personal account of her own father and his post-war suffering but then goes on to explain why 'Today I am here with my granddaughter', which makes it more authentic because the writer is speaking from her experiences. To bring her granddaughter to a dawn service shows how committed she is to the event. One way the speaker enforces the need to attend commemorations is by the quote from Bertrand Russell: 'War does not determine who is right – only who is left.' By including the words of a well-known, well-respected person, it adds weight to her argument that Anzac Day should be commemorated. The speaker and her granddaughter are part of those 'left'. **She uses Bertrand Russell's famous quote to emphasise that she and others like her all around the world are the living example of what he says. This is also a pun: 'who is right/who is left' is a play on the words 'right/left', the marching call for soldiers; and also the word 'right' meaning correct and the word 'left' meaning remnant, left over. The narratives around war and fighting are often to do with who won (or should have won), i.e. who was in 'the right', whereas the speaker is asking us to also remember those who were 'left behind' when the soldiers went to war and those who are 'left' now (descendants) of those who went to war. The effect of this is to reinforce that war has long-reaching consequences.**

By repeating the phrase 'who is left' keeps the statement to the forefront of our minds because it is an important one the speaker wants us to consider. Yes, it is good to remember the dead and those who fought for our country, but we also need to remember the friends, families and communities who were 'left behind' and the descendants and the sacrifices they made because of war. **The repetition ensures that this point is the lasting point for us, hammering home the point that by attending the services on Anzac Day, we are honouring and valuing our ancestors who fought so we could be here now.**

Finally, the speaker uses details and statistics such as 'the Aquitania with the 22nd Battalion in May 1940 ... in Greece with the 5th Field Regiment, led by Colonel Andrews, at Maleme', which adds credibility to the story by including actual dates and names of the battalions so that we understand she is speaking of real people, and real events. **Some of these names, dates and places are famous and it means that her 'right' to speak about the importance of Anzac Day is supported because of the link she has with her father who was involved in these battles. Despite it being a long time ago now, such was the impact of war on her father (and her family), she still has very clear and specific memories of that time. This also enforces the idea that the 'end of the war' does not mean the end of its effects. The speaker shows that though everyone suffers because of war, commemorations help communities connect and that we should attend our local Anzac Day service. She wants us to be mindful that though a soldier may be a hero for the things they did in the war (even those who fight today), and wear the medals as outward symbols of that action, we still need to be respectful of those who suffer depression and mental illness, so that we can help not only the returning soldiers but their families as well. One way to show this respect and to help is by commemorating Anzac Day.**

NON-FICTION 5: abridged introduction to *Once While Travelling*

Page 98

The writer communicates her views of why the book about the company Lonely Planet is worth reading through the use of listing. This is seen when she writes about her experience and lists what she's been through: 'We've learned many lessons about business, about working and living together, about taking risks, working hard and what can happen if you throw yourself at the world with open arms and a lot of curiosity, so our story encompasses all of that: travel, work and relationships.' This shows Wheeler's experience and allows the audience to see more about her, so therefore better understand her point of view. By listing all the reasons she loved travelling and what she has gained out of it, it shows the audience that this is reality and they too could go out and have these experiences. Listing ties all of these together in the audience's mind.

There are a lot of questions included in this extract ('How did you ...?' etc.), which is appropriate because when you go to a place you don't know, you ask lots of questions. **By using the types of questions travellers use, the writer is identifying the key issues and this highlights why there is a need to put a book together in one place that would answer all these questions. By providing the answers, she is fulfilling a part of what is important to her, which is to encourage others to go and see the world. Sometimes we stop ourselves from doing something new because we are afraid and often that fear comes because of the unknown. The Wheelers' books take away some of the fear and so more people will be brave and 'put their trust in all of us at Lonely Planet'.**

Another language feature the writer uses is parallel structure, in the line 'we've lived it, breathed it and loved it'. This parallel structure and repetition of the word 'it' emphasises how the Wheelers have lived, loved and literally breathed travelling. The writer has chosen to communicate her view in this way because it shows that they are somewhat professional and experts when it comes to travel, which adds credence to their writing and will make the reader want to read their book. It also makes it seem more relatable than other books about how companies started up. **People who travel are known to be adventurers, and starting a company and writing a book is taking a risk. Perhaps the reader is the type of person who would like to do something similar. The author provides a blueprint of what she did and uses the comforting, structured rhythm of parallel structure to emphasise what is needed to succeed like they have.**

The use of personal pronouns in the text such as 'Tony and I continue to travel' and 'We've learned many lessons' is effective because it makes the writing more personal. This shows the reader that the Wheelers have experienced what is being written about. Knowing this assures the reader of the authenticity of the book's content. **Wheeler sharing personal stories also assists in making both her and the company seem more friendly and approachable. This is crucial to the reader enjoying the story and wanting to learn more.**

Wheeler is hoping that people will read about her experiences and then believe they can have it too.

ISBN: 9780170424547

NON-FICTION 6: Tessa: Some Thoughts on Friendship

Pages 100–101

The writer explains why women's relationships are more unique because she wants the reader to understand that a woman can usually always call on friends who are eager to listen and can help you laugh your way through a situation. **She explains that, no matter how old you are, the need for a friend is there and when you find someone you get along with, the friendship deepens and you cherish it more and more.** One way the writer shows the uniqueness of women's relationships is by the technique of listing. For example, 'we go without those consuming waves of obsession, yearning, and fear of rejection'. This is effective, as the writer clearly states to the reader key differences between a sexual relationship and a friendship, helping the reader to understand the simplicity that goes into a woman's relationship, reminding us of how we avoid all the complications that would usually go into a romantic relationship. Another way the writer shows this is by the use of alliteration and a simile when she says 'Scanning the crowds for a face showing some sign of affinity, I felt like a lonely heart looking for a lover.'

These two techniques worked together to draw attention to the words (scan, face, show, some, sign) to develop the sense of need, or desperateness she felt at that time. Even though she has just told us the bad things of a romantic relationship, she uses the 'lonely heart' imagery to remind us that the pain or feelings are very similar. **She wants to emphasise how strongly she felt about wanting to find someone in a new town and how wonderful it was to find another woman towards whom she had a natural pull.** **This links the feeling of being alone with the longing for companionship in a loving relationship. The use of this simile also makes the reader think about how these things could be connected: that the urge for a woman to be with someone she knows is as strong as a fully developed relationship. The word choice of 'affinity', which means a natural understanding for someone or something, shows that friendships between women have an element of understanding.**

The writer wants the reader to understand how unique women's relationships are because she wants us to realise how much we should appreciate these relationships and cherish the deepening friendships we have. Finally, by including a personal anecdote, describing a situation where the two friends are in the kitchen painting, the writer is able to draw us into the story so that we witness the beginning of this friendship. They shared a physical chore ('slapped off-white over the orange medallion wallpaper') while the writer was nursing her grief over a broken relationship. The use of specific adjectives (off-white, orange, medallion) and abstract nouns (warmth, empathy, loss, hope) in this anecdote enhance the moment for the reader – as if we are there too or can remember a similar time when a friend has worked beside us in our grief. **Even the acknowledgement that their shared experienced meant different things and that's okay is highlighted in the last three words 'whiff of hope', which leaves us with a concluding and definitive view of women's relationships.**

ISBN: 9780170424547